POWER SHIFTERS

ATMOSPHERES, CLIMATES & HOW YOU CAN INFLUENCE THEM

POWER SHIFTERS
Atmospheres, Climates and How You Can Influence Them
Published by M.A.P.S. Institute, Inc.

Unless otherwise noted, all Scripture quotations are from the King James Version of the Bible.

ISBN 0972671846
Library of Congress Control Number: 2005933829

Printed in the United States of America

For further information or to order contact:
    Cornerstone Church
    P.O. Box 351690
    Toledo, OH 43635
    www.cornerstonechurch.us

Dedication

To my friends in the developing nations of the world who have done so much, with so little, for so long— your time is now!

Endorsements

"In a busy world where our time is of the essence and leisure reading has become a luxury few can afford, most of us do not have time to read every book that comes off the press. When we do read, we want the information to be fuel to the flames of our destiny provoking us to make the adjustments that accelerates the purpose of God in our lives. As a leader, as a thinker, or as a person who is set to influence their generation, I strongly encourage you to invest your time and resources in pursuit of this arsenal of wisdom. Indeed, *Power Shifters* is an excellent use of your time. It is provocative and purposeful, providing the grit and grace of a seasoned thinker whose writings deserve your undivided attention. To be sure, this book is *'a nail in a sure place!'*"

Bishop T. D. Jakes, Sr.
Senior Pastor
The Potter's House of Dallas, TX

"Power Shifters must be read by every pastor, especially those who are church planters.

I have used Pastor Pitts' teaching on Atmospheres and Climates all over the world, and I have encouraged leaders to teach these principles to their members. This book should be used as a text book in Bible Schools, as these principles are DYNAMIC."

Bishop Tudor Bismark
Founder
New Life Ministries International
Harare, Zimbabwe

"When Michael Pitts walks into a room, he lights it up with his charisma, brilliant insight, and practical knowledge. This book captures Pastor Pitts' persona. *Power Shifters* is a remarkable read! Apply its principles."

Pastor Kirbyjon Caldwell
Senior Pastor
Windsor Village United Methodist Church
Houston, TX

"I have found over the years one of the keys to ministry is displacing the negative by creating an atmosphere for growth and solutions. Michael Pitts has captured and articulated in this book the power principles necessary to change the world in which you live!"

Pastor Phil Pringle
Founder / Senior Pastor
Christian City Church
Oxford Falls, Australia

"In 25 years of pastoring and teaching I have come across very few who have the insight Michael has on how the spirit world functions. His clear understanding and boldness comes across in a dynamic and timely manner in this powerful book. Buckle up and get ready for quite a ride!"

Dick Bernal
Senior Pastor / Founder
Jubilee Christian Center
San Jose, CA

"My covenant brother, Pastor Michael Pitts, is raising his voice like a trumpet and summoning the power of God to awaken an emerging apostolic company to plunder Babylon and participate in the release of a church captured by its illusory culture and seal Babylon's ultimate doom. The day to be Spirit-sensitive is upon us again, and a generation is ready to apply the Wind-velocity of the Chariots of God, and be caught up in a power-shift under an open heaven like Ezekiel and Daniel of old. The temperature of heaven's passion in this company of power-shifters will release the precipitation of a latter rain of heaven's glory and call an acculturated and anemic church to recover the testimony of the Lord in all its fullness in the earth. We need to hear this 'Word in season' from a seasoned apostolic warrior in the Kingdom. Here's to the Power Shifters that will deconstruct a compromised culture and manifest a Kingdom culture!"

Dr. Mark J. Chironna
Senior Pastor
The Master's Touch International Church
Orlando, FL

"Pastor Michael Pitts, a seasoned fruitful pastor, a preacher who is in a class of his own, pens his incredible unique insight, his sharp prophetic revelation on the pages of his latest book, *Power Shifters*. This book is a must for all people who want to know what God is doing in and on the earth today. I don't know of more relevant, accurate, current cutting edge revelation in the Body of Christ, than the topics that Pastor Michael presents to us in his book *Power Shifters*. The revelation of this material, being invaluable to the church of the 21st Century, gives the reader the keys and the insight to influence and bring change not only to individual lives but to cities and nations. I cannot recommend Pastor Pitts and this book more highly to you. A must for Kingdom seeking believers."

Pastor Peter J. Mortlock Th.D.
Senior Pastor
City Impact Churches International
Auckland, New Zealand

Table of Contents

SECTION ONE

Climate Change

"The significant problems we face cannot
be solved at the same level we were
at when we created them."
— *ALBERT EINSTEIN*

"The desire to challenge the status quo is
the gateway to revelation."
—*MICHAEL PITTS*

Chapter One

Understanding Atmospheres, Climates and Strongholds

At the beginning of World War II, Las Vegas was a quiet, sleepy, backwater town in a lush valley in the desert of southern Nevada. Apart from a railroad stop and some mining interests, the city of less than 10,000 in population drew little attention. America's entry into the war brought the defense industry into the valley, drawn by its isolated location as well as its plentiful water and inexpensive energy due to nearby Hoover Dam.

Although the war spurred the city's growth, Las Vegas' big boom began after the war, when Benjamin "Bugsy" Siegel came to town. Acting on orders from Meyer Lansky, his boss and long-time partner in organized crime, Siegel scoped out Las Vegas' potential as a gambling center. The state of Nevada had legalized gambling in 1931 and Lansky, Siegel, and a few other underworld leaders soon recognized the much larger profit margin that legal casinos would afford.

In 1946, bankrolled by six million dollars in mob funds, "Bugsy" Siegel opened the Flamingo, the first of Las Vegas' hotel/casino operations. When it failed to turn a profit, due in part to inadequate promotion and in part to Siegel's skimming off of huge sums of construction money, Siegel was murdered and Lansky stepped in directly. Under Lansky's oversight, the Flamingo became profitable within a year. Other hotel/casinos were built: the Sands, the Thunderbird, the Desert Inn, the Sahara, the Riviera, the Stardust, the Tropicana, and Caesar's Palace. After Fidel Castro seized power in Cuba in 1959, many successful mob-owned casinos in Havana, feeling the squeeze of the new Communist government, relocated to Las Vegas. Las Vegas boomed as America's gambling mecca, an industry built almost exclusively with mob money.

The powers at the genesis of a place stamp it with a certain DNA which carries on until challenged by a power of equal or greater strength. Many mob-controlled gambling houses may have been sanitized into "gaming establishments" but the spirit of origin still at rest controls the culture of Vegas because the climate remains conducive and consistent with its original assignment.

Why do they come? What makes Las Vegas the fifth most popular vacation destination in the world for non-American travelers and its airport the seventh busiest in the world? What draws millions of people annually to this "oasis" in the desert? Is it the glitz and the glamour? Is it the neon light extravaganza on the Strip? Is it the over-the-top opulence of the resort hotels with their recreations of a volcano, the Eiffel Tower, or the Great Pyramid and Sphinx of Egypt?

By far, the vast majority of visitors—both American and non-American—who fill the hotel rooms of Las Vegas come for one reason: to gamble in the city's world-famous casinos. Most lose much more money than they win—and they *expect* to. That's one of the great ironies about the Las Vegas casino scene: most of the people who come to the city to gamble come *prepared* to lose money. Although they may hold out a hope of striking it rich, they realize that the odds are against them. After all, those big resort hotel/casino complexes don't stay in business by losing money to patrons who win big at the gaming tables! They stay in business from the millions of dollars that patrons bet—and lose—night after night.

Of course, some people do win, and some win big, but they amount to only a tiny percentage of those who play—just enough to keep people coming; just enough to keep them hoping that they could be next in the "winner's circle."

Las Vegas is such a "draw" that many people from all over the world plan *ahead of time* to lose their money. I know of people who get together with their friends and travel together, budgeting into their trip expense how much they can afford to lose at the tables or the slot machines. They expect to lose; they just don't know how long it will take. If you asked them what they are doing for their vacation, they probably would not say, "I'm going to Las Vegas and lose a lot of money," but in reality, that is what they are doing. With many of them, it is a mentality, a mindset that they never consciously question.

Why are so many people drawn to Las Vegas to gamble and lose their money? What accounts for the appeal of this industry, and of this city in particular? Is there something beyond mere adventure and the desire for excitement that draws so many people to this city? Could there be some *spiritual* motivation that draws them; a motivation of which they have no conscious awareness?

I believe the answer is yes. Many of the millions who visit Las Vegas every year are drawn by the *climate* of the city. I'm not talking about the physical climate but the *spiritual* climate. There is a *spirit* in Las Vegas that encourages high living, free spending, and gambling; a spirit that has become so entrenched that it has created a spiritual climate that pervades the entire region. That spirit took root when organized crime arrived and established an atmosphere of greed and lust for easy profits. With the building of that first hotel and casino and the free flow of mob money, that atmosphere found receptivity, which led to a second hotel, and a third, and so on.

Over time, that atmosphere developed into a climate stamped so strongly with that original negative spirit that it became a powerful enticement, an all but irresistible attraction to many people, drawing them in from everywhere outside the region. Today, that draw is so strong that it creates an atmosphere in which some people *plan* on being in agreement with that spirit even before they ever show up! The spirit of that place finds a responsive chord in their spirit that draws them to come, even from great physical distances.

Different geographical regions have different climates depending on the prevailing spirit that has established a foothold there. For example, Detroit, Michigan will always be known as "Motown," or "Motor City" because of the spirit that Henry Ford stamped on the area when he built his first automobile plant. Detroit quickly became the hub for the American automotive industry and remains so to this day.

In the 19th century John D. Rockefeller, one of America's first true business tycoons, stamped his influence on the Manhattan area of New York City as a major financial district. The climate he established still prevails today. More than ever, Wall Street represents the pulse and heartbeat—the very lifeblood—of American business, industry, and financial investments. Washington has a culture that is different from the culture of Hollywood which is different from the culture of Lagos,

Nigeria, which is different from the culture of London, Great Britain.

Some places are so inextricably linked to significant shifting events until the names become merged and synonymous. These shifting events become doorways by which a spiritual power and/or philosophy moves into the collective consciousness of an entire generation. These shifting events can so shape the culture until its effects may be felt for decades.

Woodstock was a shifting event. The festival is still known by this name even though it was never held at Woodstock. After hearing about the scheduled event local opposition arose and the concert had to be moved. Sam Yasgur prevailed upon his father Max to allow the event to be held at the family's 600 acre farm in Bethel, New York. What was billed as "Three days of fun and music" picked up momentum and developed a life of its own. It is estimated that 500,000 people attended. They were announcing the Age of Aquarius. It did not happen however in a vacuum. This was the high point—the culmination of the hippie, counterculture that had been brewing for most of the 1960's. Let me explain.

The country, especially the young were dealing with the Vietnam War which consumed the sixties like a ravenous beast. By 1969 the time of Woodstock American troop commitment would reach a staggering 550,000. Then there were the assassinations.

J.F.K.—The assassination of President John Fitzgerald Kennedy in Dallas, November 22, 1963 shattered the hopes of a nation. He was the youngest President ever elected and also the youngest to die at 46.

Malcolm X—The brilliant mind and cutting language of Malcolm was silenced on February 21, 1965 (the first day of National Brotherhood Week). He was the spokesperson for the nation of Islam and founder of the Organization of Afro-

American Unity. The distrust and frustration in America was growing.

M.L.K.—Baptist Minister, noble laureate, and civil rights activist. His incredible oratory caused a nation to listen and take notice. Martin Luther King, Jr.'s life was cut short standing on the balcony of the Loraine Motel in Memphis, Tennessee, April 4, 1968. The spokesperson for nonviolent resistance was gone. The days that followed were filled by riots and fires in major cities.

Bobby Kennedy—While campaigning for the Democratic Presidential Nomination he was shot June 6, 1968. A decade before he had made an impressive showing as the chief counsel of the Senate Labor Rackets Committee hearings in which he squared off against Jimmy Hoffa in a verbal bout that gained him much notoriety. Whatever hopes of decency the American public had left seemed to be swallowed up in his death.

Tracking with the deaths of famous leaders was a growing counterculture picking up speed and converts. The war was sucking the oxygen out of optimism. Assassins' bullets had pierced the heart of a nation; the beatniks and hippies decided to drop out.

Haight-Ashbury—The epicenter of the 60's hippie movement—named for the intersection of Haight and Ashbury, this district in San Francisco was a place where power was beginning to shift. Free love, illegal drugs, and psychedelic rock groups preached the message of alternative lifestyles. The movement had help—The Beatles.

It is interesting to note that before J.F.K.'s assassination, The Beatles had made unsuccessful attempts to break into the American music market. In 1963 on Dick Clark's American Bandstand they were actually laughed to scorn. But the climate was changing. In the weeks after J.F.K.'s death their music began getting airplay. The Beatles made three appearances in February 1964 on the Ed Sullivan Show and Beatlemania began.

One month before Woodstock Neil Armstrong would put his footprint on the moon and history July 20, 1969. For a decade shifting events were moving a culture and Woodstock would be the culmination of ten years of angst and a desire to connect with others who adhered to the message and to shift the power.

As the antiestablishment became in the ensuing years the establishment, the Woodstock children changed laws, pushed God out, wrecked havoc on marriage, morality, and the schools.

When the cup is full, when the culture is ready, when the climate is right, the power shifts!

In the same way, different spiritual climates develop over different regions of the country according to which spirits establish a foothold and gain acceptance there. Some climates are healthier and more positive than others. Places that have witnessed great movements of God's Spirit in the past, for example, often retain a residue spirit for many years, and work for the kingdom of God progresses more easily there than in other places. On the other hand, regions under a prevailing climate of oppression, bondage, blindness, and failure prove much more resistant to God's Spirit. Many people in such places live lives characterized by depression, poverty, family disintegration, crime, and an unending struggle just to survive everyday life.

These are just two examples of how the spiritual climate of a region affects the lives of everyone who lives there. Understanding the nature of prevailing atmospheres and climates is important for at least two reasons. First, it will help us learn how to identify the prevailing spirit and climate over a region. Second, it will help us understand that as Christians, both individually and corporately as the body of Christ, we have not only the calling of God but also the power to change negative spiritual climates. God has called and empowered us to tear down strongholds and infuse stale, stagnant negative spiritual climates with the fresh, vibrant, life-giving and life-changing culture of the kingdom of Heaven.

As children of God, we are called and equipped to be *power shifters* in our world—to shift power from Satan's culture of death to Christ's culture of life.

Spirits Seek a Voice

Spirits seek expression in the material world because only then can they exert their fullest influence—for good or bad—on the hearts and minds of human beings. Only then can they shape and control human culture.

All spirit powers ultimately seek manifestation in the material world. To do this they must occupy time and space. Until this is achieved they are relegated to the realm of thought, theory, philosophy or feeling. They seek to move however from concept to concrete.

To do this spirit powers must seek to produce agreement with mankind for God has made man the keeper of the earth. If man will respond in favor with the will of the powers of the air, an atmosphere is created to make the will of the spirit power more likely to occur. People then begin to give expression to the agreements they have made spiritually in tangible concrete forms. The receptivity or even passivity towards these expressions creates a climate by which the desire of spiritual influence becomes contagious. Over time a value system, philosophies, and schools of thought develop like a walled city around the intent of these principalities to protect them from ever losing their grip on the territory they lord over. This is what eventually comes to be known as culture. These cultures can entail colloquial traditions and superstitions. They can perpetuate dysfunction and cyclical patterns of failure throughout generations.

Since it is impossible to be delivered from anything we consider normal, demonic powers seek to acculturate us into a social system by which we are surrounded by a dominant culture that accepts our bondage as normal.

Remember unclean spirits seek rest. When the unclean spirit is gone out of a man, he walketh through dry places, "seeking rest," and findeth none (Matt. 12:43). Unclean powers want to be normalized and remain unchallenged. In Mark 1:23-24, Jesus met a man in the synagogue with an unclean spirit; "And he cried out, Saying, Let us alone; what have we to do with thee, thou Jesus of Nazareth? "

Now when a strong man keeps his house his goods are safe until a stronger one has come upon him (Matt. 12:29).

These are the days when power is shifting! The Holy Spirit is greater than principalities and powers of the air. The Holy Spirit is finding all over the world those who are delighting themselves with the will of God. By giving expression to His Spirit the culture of heaven is coming out of concept and theory and is occupying previously held territory in the time and space here on earth.

Our biggest challenge is making our voice—the voice of faith—stand out in the midst of the babble of other voices clamoring for the attention of the people of the world. In First Corinthians 14:10, Paul said that there are "many kinds of voices in the world, and none of them is without signification." There are many different voices in the world and every one of them is seeking to occupy time and space. Every voice, good or bad, seeks entrance into a human heart and mind, to find receptivity there so it can gain a foothold and begin establishing an atmosphere for wider acceptance.

This is an important principle to understand because all of us express in our attitude and behavior whatever spirit controls our mind. To one degree or another, we are all products of our culture. Our culture is characterized by whatever spirits or influences have become dominant. Inevitably, we will express in some way the dominant spirit in our life. We become, in a sense, walking billboards of the culture we are a part of. If we have bought into the common secular culture, our beliefs, values, attitudes, and behavior will reflect those of that culture. Quite often, just one look at people in America is enough to tell what *subculture* they belong to, whether it's the skinheads, the reggae group, the jocks, the computer nerds, the punk-rockers, or the Goths. Their dress, behavior, and lifestyle reveal the dominant voice in their lives; the prevailing spirit that controls them.

If, on the other hand, we reject the common culture in favor of another one—a Christian culture based on biblical values, for example—we may become identified as part of a *counterculture*: meaning we live in the prevailing culture but refuse to live according to the dominant values of that culture. Our position in a culture is determined by which spirit or voice we respond to and how consistently we respond to it.

A spiritual climate does not develop overnight. It strengthens over time as one particular spiritual influence gains wider and wider acceptance. It is a progression that begins with a spiritual influence that establishes an atmosphere, which then strengthens to a prevailing climate, which becomes a stronghold that becomes the architect of culture. Let's look at this progression in greater detail.

Spiritual Influence Creates Atmosphere

First of all, *response to spiritual influence creates atmosphere.* The principalities and powers in the spirit world seek to influence humanity. They can't *make* us do anything, but they try to gain an advantage over us by getting us to respond to their spiritual influence. That response creates a certain spiritual *atmosphere*.

All of us are more likely to do certain things in certain atmospheres. Have you ever walked into a place where a fight recently occurred and felt the anger in the room, even though you didn't know about the fight at the time? In that setting, did you find it easier to be argumentative yourself, even though you were in a peaceful mood before you came? If a spirit of anger is present, and we respond in kind to that spirit, we help create an atmosphere that allows the spirit of anger to continue functioning.

Our response to a spirit either strengthens or weakens its influence, depending on how we respond. This principle holds true no matter what kind of spirit we're talking about: good or bad, positive or negative. Without a word being said, we can walk into a room and feel acceptance or rejection, hostility or amity, peace or strife. Whatever spirit seems to be prevalent, our response will either feed it or starve it.

In order for a particular atmosphere to exist, someone must have already responded to the influence of a spirit conducive to that atmosphere. Once an atmosphere is established, it becomes more conducive for anyone else who enters that atmosphere to respond accordingly. We all know that it's easier to be mad around mad folks! It's easier (and more pleasant!) to be happy around happy people! It's easier to become depressed around depressed people or to have faith around faith-filled folks! If you want to be a winner, surround yourself with winners. If you want to be successful, hang around with successful people. That's how atmospheres work. According to our response, we can either give in to the prevailing atmosphere or we can shift that atmosphere. We can either be an accommodator to help sustain the existing atmosphere, or a power shifter to change it. The power is ours.

We have to understand our response to spiritual things before we can understand our initiation in spiritual things. For example, we need to understand that God is the initiator and we are the responder. This is true even in our praise. We don't initiate praise; our praise is merely a response to what God has already initiated. Psalm 150:6 says, "Let everything that hath breath praise the Lord." In other words, God gives us breath (the initiator) and we respond by praising Him. Verse 2 of the same Psalm says, "Praise him for his mighty acts: praise him according to his excellent greatness." God, the exceedingly great initiator, performs mighty acts and we, the responders, praise Him for what He has done. Even our tithe is a response to God because we are simply returning to Him one-tenth of what He has already given us.

As "the anointed cherub that covereth" (Ezek. 28:14) who once presided over the praise and worship in heaven, Lucifer is an expert with atmosphere. He is a master manipulator who knows just where to focus his energies in his efforts to influence human society. Why else, for example, would he seek to control the popular music industry? Music is a universal language and its popularity particularly among young people makes it one of the primary vehicles for shaping their beliefs, values, and worldview.

It would be hard to underestimate the importance and role of music in the life and culture of today's youth. For this reason, Satan seeks to infuse into their music his godless message of anger, antiestablishment, promiscuity, hatred, hopelessness, depression, and despair. It is human nature that eventually we become what we continually fill our minds with. Is it any surprise, then, that suicide, violence, sexual license, and addictions of all kinds afflict so many of the young people in our country today?

Few communication media affect the human spirit the way music does. Lyrics affect the mind, rhythm affects the will, and melody affects the emotions. Show me the kind of music someone listens to and I can tell you a lot about that person's lifestyle. If you fill your mind with songs about broken relationships and how "somebody done somebody wrong," don't be surprised when it comes true in your own life. If your daughter listens day and night to songs about being sexy and shaking her booty and getting it on with a guy, don't be surprised when she has a baby out of wedlock. If your son immerses himself in sad songs of suicidal despair or angry songs of thug life, don't be surprised when he commits suicide or takes a gun to school to shoot some of his classmates. Music creates an atmosphere conducive to behavior that reflects the spirit of the music.

Whatever medium is employed, unclean spirits are always working against us to persuade us to become depressed, suicidal, antisocial or to hate other people—anything that will turn us from God and sow destruction into our lives. If they can get us into an atmosphere where that kind of spirit is already being responded to, we become more likely to respond in that same way than we would in a different environment.

The reverse is also true. If the Spirit of God can draw us into an atmosphere where He is already being responded to, we are more likely to receive His peace, love, blessings, and joy in that atmosphere than in another setting. Atmosphere is a response to spiritual influence.

Atmosphere Sustained Creates Climate

Just as a sustained response to a particular spiritual influence creates an atmosphere, *atmosphere that is sustained creates climate*. A climate is stronger than an atmosphere. It means that the atmosphere has become pervasive. One cold day in Florida does not change the climate of the state. Cold weather may indicate an aberration, a temporary atmospheric disruption, but the climate of Florida remains semitropical. Likewise, one hot December day in Ohio does not change Ohio's climate. Physical climate is determined by the pervasive weather conditions in a region. Winter climate in Ohio is cold despite the occurrence of a few unseasonably warm days. The prevailing atmosphere is one of cold weather.

Climate means that the atmosphere is predictable. It is unlikely to change significantly and any changes that do occur are generally very small and of short duration. Predictability also means that certain things are more likely to grow in certain climates than in others. Florida's climate is well-suited for raising citrus fruit, but someone who tried to grow oranges or grapefruit in Ohio would be taking a great risk. Ohio's climate is not conducive for citrus fruit, which requires long periods of warm weather and lots of sunshine.

It's the same way with the things of the Spirit: certain things grow best in certain climates. The spiritual climate in an area depends on which spiritual atmosphere is pervasive. Many times, even seemingly large moves of the Spirit of God throughout a region have turned out to be only climatic disruptions. They did not usher in a climate of blessing or freedom because the pervasive negative atmosphere of ungodliness was not displaced.

It is not enough simply to go into a strong negative spiritual climate and preach the gospel. Certainly, the Word of God is living and active and sharper than a two-edged sword and is powerful to change lives, but to change the entire climate in a place usually involves active spiritual warfare as well. This is because the negative spiritual climate must not only be opposed but displaced and supplanted by the positive climate of God's Spirit. An entrenched negative climate will not yield without a fight, and waging that battle is part of what the church of Jesus Christ is called to do.

Just as the natural climate varies from place to place, so does the spiritual climate. Reaching people for Christ is easier in some places than in others. The message of the gospel may be welcomed openly and joyfully in one location and be vigorously opposed and persecuted in another.

We know the incredible power of the seed of God's Word to produce. However Jesus taught that the soil into which the seed is sown into can determine its level of productivity. If we take the parable found in Matthew (13:3-9, 18-23) and we liken the soil to the climate the seed is sown into we can gain fresh insight. After all who could argue against the truth that the same message (seed) preached in different locations (climate) has differing degrees of results (30, 60, 100 fold). If the soil has become hardened and resistant to the seed there must come an anointing to plow—to break the agreements of unclean spirits to produce an openness to the seed (more on this later).

Climate Sustained Creates Strongholds

The relationship between a negative spiritual climate and the hardness of human hearts leads to the next step in the progression: *climate that is sustained creates strongholds*. Strongholds have to do with the way people think. A stronghold is an entrenched mindset that colors how a person thinks and feels about himself, others, God, and the world around him. It also shapes how he behaves and responds to that world.

Paul told the Corinthians:

> [4](*For the weapons of our warfare are not carnal, but mighty through God to the pulling down of strongholds;) [5]Casting down imaginations, and every high*

thing that exalteth itself against the knowledge of God, and bringing into captivity every thought to the obedience of Christ (2 Corinthians 10:4-5).

This passage is the only New Testament occurrence of the word "strongholds," and Paul is referring to strongholds of the mind. He describes the pulling down of strongholds as "casting down *imaginations* and every *high thing* that exalteth itself against the knowledge of God."

It's amazing how some people think, what some people's concept of "normal" is. All of us are raised in certain climates and taught how to respond to certain atmospheres, which is actually yielding to the spiritual influence. The processes we learn and the methods we use to cope with our climate are the things we build our lives around, and they become strongholds for us. For those who grow up in a negative spiritual climate, the strongholds of their minds become the walls of a prison cell and holds them in bondage to the particular spirit that they have responded to.

Once in place, a stronghold may last for generations and even be passed down in families. We see this time and again in families who have generation after generation of alcoholics, or generation after generation of poverty, or divorce, or premature death, or some other kind of dysfunction. The stronghold becomes such a part of their family history that eventually they look on it as "normal" for their family. They rarely question it but simply accept it as "the way things are." And so the stronghold perpetuates.

Sometimes a stronghold takes the form of "limitation thinking," where a person believes himself or herself to be limited by what other people have said: "You can't do that"; "you shouldn't do that"; "that's for others, not you"; "who do you think you are, trying to rise above your station?"; "you'll never get a good education"; "you'll never have a good job"; "you'll never have a happy marriage"; "quit trying to think"; "don't forget where you came from."

After awhile, those kinds of thoughts get into your brain and even if you move away from those who fed them to you all your life, you will still have that limitation thinking in your mind. It will hold you back until you learn to bring down that stronghold and replace it with God's "possibility thinking." That's why Paul talks in Second Corinthians 10:5 about "bringing into captivity *every thought* to the obedience of Christ." Furthermore, he says in Romans 12:2, "Be not conformed to this world: but be ye transformed by the renewing of your mind, that ye may prove what is that good, and acceptable, and perfect, will of God." The purpose of all of this is so that we may have the "mind of Christ" (1 Cor. 2:16).

Having the mind of Christ is the opposite of being bound by strongholds. Instead of being bound up by strongholds, we tear them down in the power of Christ. Strongholds by their very nature are deeply rooted and firmly entrenched and do not give way easily. Sometimes, removing a stronghold may seem like an impossible task. The Bible says that nothing is impossible with God (Luke 1:37) and that we can do all things through Christ, who strengthens us (Phil. 4:13).

Strongholds Sustained Determine Culture

Response to spiritual influence creates atmosphere, sustained atmosphere creates climate, and sustained climate creates strongholds. This leads to the final stage in the process: *strongholds sustained determine culture*. In other words, the culture we live in is determined by the mindsets that control the way we think. Collectively as a nation of people, the strongholds of our mind shape the beliefs, assumptions, values, customs, ethics, and mores of our society.

Culture is the totality of socially transmitted behavior patterns, arts, beliefs, institutions and all other products of human work and thought. To one extent or another, we are all products of our culture. It touches every arena of our lives. Socially transmitted behavior simply means that we know what to think, what to do, and how to act because of what others have passed on to us. We know what is acceptable and unacceptable behavior because of the standards transmitted by our parents, grandparents, and other recognized authority figures of an earlier generation.

Worldwide, cultures differ from place to place and region to region. Generally speaking, cultural standards vary widely between groups. Many variables factor into this broad diversity of cultures: geography, physical climate, ethnicity, religion, level of industrialization. Because any culture is strongly affected by the strongholds in the minds of its people, the fact that strongholds differ from one location to the next also helps account for the cultural diversity we see in the world.

As products of our culture, we tend to accept as "normal" any attitudes, values, or behaviors that are in line with that culture. Anything that does not line up with our accepted standards of behavior we generally condemn as abnormal, wrong, or even evil. Sometimes standards differ even within regions of a particular culture. In the United States, for example, many Christians, particularly in the "Bible Belt" of the South, are taught to believe that consumption of alcoholic beverages of any kind to any degree is a sin. In other parts of the country and in many nations around the world, social drinking in moderation is a perfectly acceptable practice. It's a cultural thing.

Here's another example. Many Christians have been raised in a culture that either states or implies that the people of God ought to be depressed and sad and broke and quiet and uneducated and unskilled and powerless; marginalized on the fringes of society, safely tucked away from any chance of becoming a nuisance to everybody else. "Let the Christians do their thing in their churches and we'll do our thing over here and everything will be fine as long as they stay put." Unfortunately, too many Christians have bought into that cultural mindset and accepted it as *normal*. The image of a marginalized, powerless, irrelevant church has become a stronghold in their minds.

Why is it okay for everybody to prosper except Christians? Who says it's *normal* for believers to struggle financially day after day? Why is it okay for Christians to go to a sporting event and laugh and shout and scream and hoot and holler with the best of them, but when they come to church they're supposed to sit quietly with their hands in their laps? Why is it okay to speak passionately about sports or politics or hobbies but not about Jesus Christ?

All of these are common strongholds that have become embedded in our culture in many places and, often, in the minds of believers. Strongholds seek to keep people in bondage, and because sustained strongholds determine culture, culture serves to help perpetuate the bondage.

The evil spirits, principalities, and powers of the air seek to bind up people and entire regions and are always working to bring their influence out of the spirit realm and into the material realm. There are many voices in the land and none of them fails to convey a message, whether it be suicide or oppression or racism or hatred or war or poverty or whatever else it may be.

All these spirits try to influence, but someone must respond. If enough people respond to a spirit, an atmosphere is created that, if sustained, grows into a climate and then a stronghold that can keep generations of people in bondage. That's when the spirit begins to take influence over entire cities and nations and regions until they begin to hold even God's people in captivity.

The end result is a culture in which the principalities and powers of the air become the "gods" of this world, deceiving people into pursuing wealth and pleasure and any number of other things as the keys to happiness rather than pursuing the one true and living God, in whom alone true happiness is found. We can see it in Las Vegas and New Orleans and any number of other places. The principalities and powers begin exercising illegitimate authority over the nation until wrong is called right and right is called wrong; until good people are looked on as evil and evil people regarded as heroes.

It is time for a change. The time has come for a great *power shift*. God is ready to raise up some people who will learn how to pull down strongholds and, ultimately, change the culture in which they live. Those people are *us*, the children of God, the body of Christ. He has called us to change the climate, tear down the strongholds, and confront our culture with the transforming power of the gospel of Jesus Christ.

Are you up to the challenge? Say yes!

Acceptable religion is not a compromise; it is a victory for the enemy.

"A city that is set on an hill cannot be hid." — Matthew 5:14

Chapter Two

Confronting Our Culture

We are called to tear down strongholds!

By and large, the cultures of the earth are under the dominance of the powers of darkness. The principalities and powers of the air hold billions of people around the world in spiritual bondage and blindness. Demonic strongholds are firmly entrenched all over the world. In many places, these strongholds have held sway for decades; centuries, in some cases.

Jesus came to break down strongholds and set captives free. He described His mission in these words:

> *18 The Spirit of the Lord is upon me, because he hath anointed me to preach the gospel to the poor; he hath sent me to heal the brokenhearted, to preach deliverance to the captives, and recovering of sight to the blind, to set at liberty them that are bruised, 19 to preach the acceptable year of the Lord* (Luke 4:18-19).

As Head of the Church, Christ has commissioned and anointed us, His body, to do the same. He has charged us to carry the conflict right into the enemy's camp. Jesus said that the gates of hell would not prevail against His Church. Our mission is to storm the very gates of hell, Satan's headquarters. That means we have to take on his strongholds, and tackling the devil's strongholds means we have to confront the culture in which they manifest.

If we are called to demolish strongholds, why is it that we see so few of them coming down? One reason is that the church, in large measure, has all but aborted its mission. Instead of assaulting the enemy's strongholds by confronting the culture, many churches, including many who appear to be flourishing, have made *peace* with the culture. They have struck an uneasy treaty with the enemy without authorization from their Commander-in-Chief. These churches flourish because they have learned how to be successful *in* the culture, rather than standing in opposition to it. After all, why fight it when you can join it?

Despite their appearance of life and vitality, churches that flourish by accommodating the dominant culture have lost their way. First, they have either forgotten or abandoned their commission from Christ to make disciples of all the nations (Matt. 28:19-20). Instead, they focus on their own survival and "success" by compromising their principles and cooperating with the secular culture. They "go along to get along." Some of these churches have bought into liberal and unbiblical theology or doctrines that have led them down the wrong path. Many other churches have simply gotten tired of the fight. It's easier to make concessions than to continue to stand in the gap.

Second, these churches have forgotten the definition of *true* success. They think they are successful because their building is full every week. But if their "success" is due to people who continually respond to the wrong spirit and are held captive under mental strongholds of the dominant culture, they become nothing more than a reflection of that culture with no power (or desire) to challenge or change. Accommodating churches have no power to challenge the dominant culture because they have become, by their accommodation, merely a subculture to the dominant culture, espousing the same core values and beliefs of that culture while cloaking them in traditional and familiar religious and biblical language. Such churches have been sidelined and marginalized.

True success in the spirit comes not by giving in and being *received* by the culture, but in standing firm and confronting and changing the culture through the power of God. The Church is not supposed to be a subculture. We're supposed to be a *counterculture.*

There are lawless areas of the country where churches prosper because they don't challenge the lawlessness of the people. Their attitude is, "Do whatever you want to do, just come and be a part. Pray if you want to. Give if you want to. Just hang out if you want to." They draw a lot of people because they place no demands on them. Never is a word said about changing the culture; after all, they are a product of the culture. These churches make it easy—dangerously and deceptively easy—to "be" a Christian and to "serve" God. No cost or sacrifice is involved. These are houses of excuses.

In areas where a climate of superstition prevails, some churches play on and prey upon the superstitions of the people, thereby strengthening the superstitious climate. Rather than battling that climate and striving to tear down that stronghold, these churches accommodate the climate and end up building a religious system of superstition. In so doing, they simply trade one form of bondage for another and remain under the same stronghold.

Most of America's cities are at least somewhat closed to the Spirit of God. When the climate of an area is closed to God's Spirit, the end result is tired churches and weak Christians. Instead of dynamic worship and life-changing ministry, they settle for "acceptable religion." Acceptable religion comes about when a church succumbs to the dominant culture and replaces its God-ordained and Spirit-filled ministries with bland and lifeless programs that are "acceptable" to the prevailing spirits of their region. Instead of standing firm and fighting in the spirit, they capitulate and make an agreement with the powers of darkness.

This agreement is a mutual non-interference pact that goes something like this: "We won't bother you if you don't bother us." The only problem is that the devil is a liar and never lives up to his agreements. First he tries to sideline a church; then, he tries to destroy it.

Acceptable religion is not a compromise; it is a victory for the enemy. It has no power to destroy strongholds. It casts no fear into the hosts of darkness. It inflicts no damage on the devil or his works. It has no agitation value in the spirit. It does not make the things that bind us uncomfortable. It does not make the Spirit of God welcome. Acceptable religion is a form of godliness that denies the very power thereof.

One thing the Spirit of God wants to do in us is challenge our thinking and push us beyond our comfort level so that we will not settle for being a subculture that merely reflects the culture of our community, but rise up to become a counterculture in the midst of our community.

Christianity is not a subculture but a counterculture, with a totally different value system from that of the world. That is why churches and individual believers who seriously try to follow Christ often find themselves at odds with conventional thought. Christian culture is centered on the Word of God, which does not fit into any secular human culture in the world. God's Word stands in stark contrast to the values, beliefs, and practices of the world's cultures. It is this contrast that makes Christianity a counterculture.

What Time Is It?

When Jesus established His Church, He gave us the authority to bind, to loose, and to tear down strongholds. He also commissioned us to go into the world and make disciples—disciplined ones—in every nation. In order to carry out our assignment effectively, we need to learn to discern climates and times and seasons. We need to know what time it is in the spirit.

Jesus emphasized the importance of this kind of discernment during a confrontation He had with His enemies:

> *¹The Pharisees also with the Sadducees came, and tempting desired him that he would show them a sign from heaven. ²He answered and said unto them, When it is evening, ye say, It will be fair weather: for the sky is red. ³And in the morning, It will be foul weather to day: for the sky is red and lowering. O ye hypocrites, ye can discern the face of the sky; but can ye not discern the signs of the times? ⁴A wicked and adulterous generation seeketh after a sign; and there shall no sign be given unto it, but the sign of the prophet Jonas. And he left them, and departed* (Matthew 16:1-4).

God is a God of times and seasons. Ecclesiastes 3:1 says that there is a season for everything and a time for every purpose under heaven. The Israelites learned through their own experience in history that when God's time for something arrived, He brought it to pass. Whether blessing or curse, deliverance or judgment, it happened without exception. Galatians 4:4 says that, "Jesus was born when the fullness of the time was come." When Jesus began His public ministry, His message was simple: "The time is fulfilled, and the kingdom of God is at hand: repent ye, and believe the gospel" (Mark 1:15). At one point, when some of Jesus' enemies sought to seize Him, no one laid hold of Him because His "hour was not yet come" (John 7:30).

The Bible promises times of refreshing: "Repent ye therefore, and be converted, that your sins may be blotted out, when the times of refreshing shall come from the presence of the Lord" (Acts 3:19). It promises a time of reaping: "And let us not be weary in well doing: for in due season we shall reap, if we faint not" (Gal. 6:9). "Due season" is when everybody gets what's due them! Even the devil has a season, and his time is growing short: "For the devil is come down unto you, having great wrath, because he knoweth that he hath but a short time" (Rev. 12:12b). If that was written 2000 years ago, think how much shorter his time is now!

We know then that there are times and seasons. But the times and seasons in the spiritual realm do not always coincide with the times and seasons of the natural realm anymore than the spiritual climate coincides with the natural climate. This is one reason why people get confused or upset because they don't know what to do with the things of God. They feel frustrated because their life is uncoordinated with the season God has them in. Inner conflict arises because they are trying to do one thing while God is doing another.

Do you know what time it is? I'm referring to the time in the spirit. God has a time and a season for every one of us. Ecclesiastes 3:11 says, "He hath made everything beautiful in his time." Not only is there a time for each of us, but there is also a time for everything that is for us. Our challenge is to understand the timings and the seasons of God and how they relate to spiritual climates.

This is where the Sadducees and Pharisees had a problem. Jesus asked them, "Why is it that you can look into the sky and predict the weather, but cannot look into the spirit and discern the signs of the times? You are the religious leaders of Israel; why can't you understand what season it is in the spirit? Don't you know what time it is?"

It was because the Pharisees and Sadducees were not spiritually sensitive that they demanded that Jesus show them a sign from heaven. Jesus responded that a "wicked and adulterous generation seeketh after a sign." Instead of exercising faith, these religious leaders wanted to see a spectacle. They wanted to have their eyes dazzled rather than their hearts changed, and Jesus saw right through their hypocrisy. He told them that the only sign they would receive was the sign of Jonah. By this, Jesus was referring to His own death and resurrection, in that just as Jonah spent three days in the belly of the fish, so Jesus would spend three days buried in the tomb and then rise again.

Jesus said that those who seek a sign are part of a "wicked and adulterous generation." He was referring to spiritual adultery, or unfaithfulness to God. The Pharisees and Sadducees were the religious leaders and experts of the Jewish people. They were supposed to set the example of faithfulness for everyone else to follow. Instead, they had abandoned the true faith for a religion of rules without spirit, a form of godliness that denied the power thereof. Jesus' point is that those who are without faith seek a sign; those who have faith need no sign. For the faithful, the Word—the promise—of God is enough. Because of their lack of faith, the Pharisees and Sadducees could not understand the season they were in. They could not discern the spiritual climate. As a result, they missed the "time of [their] visitation" (Luke 19:44) and rejected the One for whom their entire religious system looked and waited.

Natural Seasons vs. Spiritual Seasons

The religious leaders of Jesus' day lacked discernment. Because they were out of touch with God, they had no idea what He was doing. Despite their great religious and scriptural knowledge, they could not discern the "signs of the times."

Throughout the Bible we see that climate has a lot to do with what God is up to. In the Old Testament, for example, a natural drought often is related to spiritual withholding or a dry season in the spirit. Deuteronomy chapter 28 describes the blessings that God's people will receive for being faithful and obedient, as well as the curses that will fall on them if they are unfaithful and disobedient. Verse 12 says, "The Lord shall open unto thee his good treasure, the heaven to give the rain unto thy land in his season, and to bless all the work of thine hand: and thou shalt lend unto many nations, and thou shalt not borrow." Rain coming upon the land, then, spoke to the people that the blessings of God were now available; He was pouring out His favor. Obedience opened the windows of heaven. The rain fell and the harvest came in. Disobedience shut up the heavens so that no rain fell and their harvest withered in the field. The physical climate often reflected the condition of the people's relationship with God.

In the New Testament we learn that God gave us these examples as symbols of spiritual realities. Under the new covenant in Christ, we can no longer interpret the times and seasons from an Old Testament point of view. Physical realities do not always reflect spiritual conditions. In Old Testament times, natural disasters were regarded as judgments from God, and sometimes they were. It is different today. Just because a flood occurs somewhere or an earthquake or tsunami devastates a region does not necessarily mean that God is angry with the people there. The natural climate doesn't always coincide now with the spiritual climate any more than natural time necessarily coincides with spiritual time.

When Jesus said, "A wicked and adulterous generation seeketh after a sign," He was saying, in effect, "Take your eyes off of natural things. Focus on the spiritual. If you can look at the sky and tell the weather, you ought to be able to see in the spirit and discern the time and the climate that you are in." He spoke of "discerning" the signs of the times, or the spiritual climate. What this means is that if we have to "discern" the spiritual climate, not only does it not coincide with the natural season, it probably collides with it! In other words, we cannot expect to understand what God is doing simply by examining the physical or natural dimension. We must dig deeper, in order to learn what is happening at the spiritual level. One of the reasons many people do not understand the timing of God and the spiritual season is because those things collide with and are, many times, the opposite of the climate in the world.

I believe that God wants to release people in the earth who have the ability to change the spiritual climate by discerning the time that they are in. God did not call us just to know and to complain about the world in which we live; He called us to change the world. We are God's appointed history-makers; we are His anointed world-changers.

When the spiritual climate is warm and receptive to the power of God, His power is unhindered and His Word penetrates into people's hearts. Praise goes forth. Miracles occur. Faith rises up. Nonbelievers come to Christ and believers grow stronger spiritually. In this kind of climate, entire cities can be turned around.

Climate equals soil quality, and soil quality affects how well the seed, or the message of the gospel, will be received. This is one of the important truths in Jesus' parable of the sower and the seed. The seed is always the same—the Word of God—but the level of the final harvest is determined by the soil quality or climate in which it is planted. Too often we focus so much attention on the seed (our message) that we give little or no attention to conditioning the soil. If we want to see our cities transformed by the power of the gospel, we have to do more than just preach it and teach it; we have to deal with the climate in which we are sowing it! And that means dealing with strongholds. If we want to see a power shift, we have to get involved with climate change.

God is ready and waiting to release into the earth a people who will possess the faith to stand against the powers of darkness and, in the power of the Holy Spirit, bring about climate change.

The human race is caught up in a raging spiritual war that most aren't even aware of. People don't act the way they act or think the way they think without reason. No matter how much we might regard ourselves to be freethinkers, none of us came up with our personal system of beliefs and values all on our own. We are products of our culture. Because of the culture we have been raised in, we believe certain things and think certain ways. By and large, that culture is under the dominant influence of the principality and power of the air. Consequently, many of our thoughts and beliefs run contrary to the Word and will of God.

That's why the Bible says that when we get saved we have to renew our minds according to the Word of God, because we have been taught lies. We believe wrong things about ourselves, about God, and about other people. But the Word of God is quick and powerful to break down those strongholds in our minds and to retrain our thinking to understand that God is for us and not against us. No matter that the prevailing climate may suggest otherwise, greater is He that is in us than he that is in the world!

We Are a Counterculture

We must learn how to discern the signs of the times because God is looking for people He can release into the world who will be in agreement with His Spirit. That is our purpose and calling as Christians. That is why Jesus Christ established the Church, His body on earth. When we get in agreement on earth with what God has proclaimed in the heavens, we will stamp our world with the power of the Holy Spirit!

Christ did not call us to sit and ease our way into heaven. He didn't call us to pray faithless, half-hearted prayers. He didn't call us to tie a knot in the end of our rope and hang on, or circle the wagons, or hold the fort until He comes to rescue us. Jesus called us to be salt and light! He called us to dispel the darkness! He called us to a militant lifestyle! He called us to be a counterculture! He called us to proclaim, "Thy Kingdom come! Thy will be done on earth as it is in heaven."

Our calling is to stand strong as a counterculture for Christ in the midst of a culture dominated by the enemy. We are to become walking billboards for the Spirit of the Living God. Jesus called it signs and wonders. Every one of us is a sign and a wonder of God's amazing grace. We are a city that is set on a hill for all to plainly see. Wherever we go, something should iterate out from us that proclaims to the world that we are a counterculture. We are in this world but are not of it. We live in a crooked system but are not crooked. We live in a hate-filled world but are not filled with hate. We are in the midst of a storm but refuse to allow the storm to be in us! We have joy in the midst of sorrow and plenty in the midst of famine.

God has called us, anointed us, and commissioned us to pull down strongholds, to set captives free, to release the bound and the oppressed, and to preach the gospel faithfully in our generation and release it into our cities and towns and set generations free from the bondage of the devil. He has called us to change the culture. The only way to change the culture is by standing against it and presenting a viable alternative. That is why we must be a counterculture. The prefix "counter" means to go against. We cannot change the culture by going along with it; we must go against it! We must "cut against the grain."

Like every other spirit, the Holy Spirit seeks ultimate expression in the earth. In order for this to happen, the will of God must occupy time and space. This occurs as we, the people of God, respond to the Spirit of God. When we respond to the Spirit of God we create an atmosphere in which He can work. Sustained long enough, that atmosphere creates a climate, which leads to strongholds—new, godly strongholds to replace the old, ungodly strongholds that are torn down in the power of the Spirit. These new strongholds, once firmly implanted and sustained, eventually will change the culture. When strongholds change, culture changes.

When we respond to the Holy Spirit, we create an atmosphere of blessing. Sustained blessing creates a climate where God has free reign. In such a climate, whole generations of people will rise up under a new stronghold of blessing and create a new culture in which our sons and our daughters prophesy; in which blessings flow like a river; in which the outlaw spirits of depression and anxiety flee. When we respond to the Holy Spirit, we create an environment in which He can find expression in time and space.

Part of the Church's problem today is that we are too busy trying to find ways to get our message accepted in the culture when we have not successfully gained entrance for it to be heard. The important thing is to get the message out as often as we can in as many different ways as we can to as many people as we can. Acceptance of our message cannot come until the message is heard widely and often. Many will reject it, but some will receive it, and that is when acceptance begins. One here, another there, then another, and another, until the message begins to take root in the community.

Advertisers live by this principle. They know that many, perhaps even most, of the people who hear or see their ads will not respond. That's okay; they are trying to find the ones who will respond. They are seeking to gain entrance, and they do it by getting the message out over and over, everywhere they can.

Satan operates the same way. He understands well how the human mind operates. He just starts throwing his message out there and doesn't care if 99 out of 100 people say, "That's weird!" Eventually, someone will say, "Okay," and gravitate towards it. All the devil is after initially is to gain entrance. Once he has entrance, he has expression in time and space and can build toward acceptance. That is why he has so carefully targeted the media and the educational system of our land. He knows that if he can get his message out through the entertainers and the journalists as well as through the people who teach our children, he can control the culture.

We in the Church, however, have not understood the power of our message, and therefore we tend to wait until somebody accepts it before we really open it up. We will never change the culture with that approach. Our job is to proclaim from the mountaintops what we have heard in secret; to get the gospel message out anyway we can: on radio, on television, in the marketplace, in the schools, in the neighborhoods, on the internet, through music, through drama. Anywhere and everywhere; just get the message out.

Don't worry about not being accepted. We're not trying to be accepted; we're trying to gain entrance. We're trying to open a door, because eventually we will find someone who will hear and accept our message. They will join with us and a stronghold will weaken and a crack will form in the wall of the prevailing culture. Soon after, somebody else will join up. The stronghold will get weaker still and the crack will widen. Before long there will be 10, then 20, then 40, then 50. After awhile, it grows to 100, then 200, then 500, then 1000, then 2000, then 3000... and that's when the culture begins to shift. Strongholds start to fall and the blessings of God begin to come and reclaim the region.

Too long we have waited for an environment where we are accepted before we ever open our mouths. Too long have the corrupt and warped values and deceptions of the devil monopolized the marketplace of ideas in our culture. Truth is the only antidote for falsehood. Accepted or not, it's time for us to open our mouths and speak the truth to a culture deceived by lies.

Buy the Truth and Sell it Not

Much of the power struggle in our culture today between those who defend traditional values and those who want to overturn them centers around the question of *truth*. What is truth? Where is truth found? Is truth absolute or does it depend on the situation or on the attitude or perception of the individual? These are questions of the ages. Man has been asking these questions for as long as he has been walking on the earth.

"What is truth?" This was Pilate's response to Jesus' statement that He had come to bear witness to the truth (John 18:37-38). It's a fair question. It's also a very important question because Jesus said that knowledge of the truth would make us free (John 8:32). Deep in our heart, we all want to know the truth. Everybody needs the assurance that some things in life are dependable. This question of truth is particularly important for the church because we must be clear on the nature and source of truth if we hope to become image changers and power shifters in our culture.

Some people believe that truth is *relative*, meaning that truth depends on the situation and the individual. What is true for one person is not necessarily true for another. In this view, there is no such thing as empirical, objective truth that applies at all times in all places to all people. In essence, truth then becomes merely that which is convenient for the moment. Relative truth means we make truth what we need it to be at any given time.

Closely related to relative truth is *subjective* truth: truth becomes simply whatever we want it to be. Subjective truth depends on our feelings. This is the philosophy of many of today's talk shows. One of the ground rules for many of these programs is that you can't challenge anybody's perspective on truth because if they believe it strongly enough, then it must be true, at least to them. Subjective feelings become more important than objective standards as determinants of truth.

Our politically correct society insists that we should not "tell the truth" if it hurts somebody's feelings. Considering how someone will feel about what we say becomes more important than the truth of what we say. This attitude has filtered into our public education system nationwide resulting in children graduating from school functionally illiterate because teachers were more concerned about them feeling good than about them learning something. They refuse to give bad grades for fear of making students feel bad or becoming emotionally scarred or damaging their self-esteem. Which is more damaging: to give a student a low grade as an incentive to work harder or for that same student to be turned down for job after job because he or she cannot read well enough to fill out the job application?

There are still others who believe that truth is a matter of consensus. Truth is whatever the majority of people say it is. By this view, even a lie can become the truth if enough people are persuaded to believe it. Therein lies the fallacy: truth can be made into a lie through distortion and misrepresentation, but no amount of manipulation or verbal gymnastics can ever turn a lie into the truth. All that results from such an attempt is self-delusion.

Considering all these different viewpoints on truth, is it any wonder that we live in a world of confusion and darkness? Our children don't know right from wrong because nobody is allowed to speak the truth anymore. Many churches and preachers have sold out the truth in an effort to become more accepted by society and draw in more people. They have traded their God-given commission as a prophetic voice *to* the culture in favor of becoming the accommodating voice *of* the culture. Gone is any proclamation of biblical truth. Gone is any kind of challenge to the people to uphold biblical morality. Gone is any emphasis on the biblical teaching regarding money and financial stewardship. Gone are any demands for repentance of sin and personal faith and commitment of life as prerequisites for following Christ. In an effort to be popular, these churches have sold their soul. By abandoning biblical truth they have left themselves with no workable standard. If nothing is prohibited, everything becomes acceptable. Because they are willing to stand for anything they become subject to falling for everything.

God's people are called to be *lovers* of truth. The Bible tells us to speak the truth to each other *in love* (Eph. 4:15). Truth is supreme. Jesus didn't come to tell "feel good" stories. He didn't come to produce a "feeling" in us. He didn't come to make the truth "relative" to certain contexts. Jesus came bringing truth—period. He even said, "I am the way, *the truth*, and the life: no man cometh unto the Father, but by me" (John 14:6 emphasis added). Truth is involved in our access to God, so we'd better know what it is!

Truth: Bought or Borrowed?

One vitally important question we need to ask ourselves regarding truth is whether we are *buying* the truth or merely *borrowing* the truth. A trivial difference? Not at all. *Bought* truth is truth we *own*; *borrowed* truth is truth that we do not own. Understanding the distinction between bought truth and borrowed truth may make the difference between success and failure or even between life and death.

Let's look at three different Scripture passages and then tie them together.

Buy the truth, and sell it not; also wisdom, and instruction, and understanding (Prov. 23:23).

¹And the sons of the prophets said unto Elisha, Behold now, the place where we dwell with thee is too strait for us. ²Let us go, we pray thee, unto Jordan, and take thence every man a beam, and let us make us a place there, where we may dwell. And he answered, Go ye. ³And one said, Be content, I pray thee, and go with thy servants. And he answered, I will go. ⁴So he went with them. And when they came to Jordan, they cut down wood. ⁵But as one was felling a beam, the axe head fell into the water: and he cried, and said, Alas, master! for it was borrowed. ⁶And the man of God said, Where fell it? And he showed him the place. And he cut down

a stick, and cast it in thither; and the iron did swim.
⁷Therefore said he, Take it up to thee. And he put out
his hand, and took it (2 Kings 6:1-7).

And now also the axe is laid unto the root of the trees:
therefore every tree which bringeth not forth good fruit
is hewn down, and cast into the fire (Matt. 3:10).

Proverbs 23:23 tells us two things: *buy the truth* and *sell it not.* Truth is valuable enough to buy no matter the cost and priceless enough to keep no matter the cost. In other words, buy the truth at any price and once you own it, hold onto it for all you've got!

The passage from Second Kings illustrates the danger and inadequacy of borrowed truth. The "sons of the prophets" apparently felt too restricted or confined living with Elisha, so they proposed building their own houses near the Jordan. Perhaps they found Elisha's standard of holy and ethical living a bit too constricting for their taste and decided to get themselves some "breathing room." Or perhaps they felt they needed no more training and were ready to be on their own. At any rate, Elisha agreed to their request and went with them to watch them build. As one of them was chopping down a tree, the axe head he was using fell into the water, and the man lamented to Elisha, "Alas, master! For it was borrowed."

Borrowed truth. In this account the axe head is a word picture representing the sharp edge of the prophetic voice, and the sons of the prophets had lost it. Proverbs 27:17 says that iron sharpens iron just as one man sharpens another. The axe head is the prophetic "edge" that it takes to cut down the "tree" of ignorance and error. Some people can't see the forest for the trees; they can't see the truth because of all the confusing and conflicting ideologies of man that surround them. The axe head has to have a sharp edge if it's ever going to clear a path through the forest. It takes the sharp edge of the prophetic voice of the people of God to cut through the underbrush and expose the truth.

Once the sons of the prophets separated themselves from Elisha and from the anointing that was on his life, they lost the sharp edge of their prophetic voice, as when the axe head fell into the water. The "sons of the prophets" appear several times in the Old Testament and never in a very positive light. They are the ones being taken by a creditor or hassling Elisha about the "double portion" of the anointing or consistently failing to understand what the prophet was doing. As a matter of fact, in this regard they are very similar to the disciples of Jesus: slow to learn and slow to comprehend.

The sons of the prophets lost their edge because they tried to live on *borrowed* truth—truth they had never paid for and made their own. They represent all the people who know all the right things to say, who have heard the truth and can even repeat it back, but do not own it. Another illustration of this is found in Acts 19:14-16 where seven sons of Sceva, a Jewish chief priest, tried to exorcise a demon by calling on the name of "Jesus whom Paul preacheth." The evil spirit answered, "Jesus I know, and Paul I know, but who are ye?" Then the demon-possessed man attacked the seven would-be exorcists and they fled, bloodied and beaten. Those seven sons of Sceva failed because they were acting on borrowed truth—truth they did not own for themselves.

Before we can speak the truth to anyone in an authoritative manner, we must *buy* the truth and make it our own. One reason so many churches fail to make a difference in their communities is because they preach borrowed truth: truth they have never really appropriated for themselves by faith and experience. Theory alone is not enough to reach people. They must see and hear the "sharp edge" of truth lived out in practical ways and demonstrated in power. The only way we can have that sharp edge is to buy the truth—to invest our lives in it—and make it our own.

In Matthew 3:10, the third of our Scripture passages, John the Baptist also spoke of an axe, saying that it was laid to the root of the trees, ready to cut down every tree that did not bear good fruit. John never lost his "sharp edge." His message always cut right to the heart of people's lives, not to damage but to heal, to correct, and to prepare their hearts for the Messiah, who would soon come in the person of Jesus of Nazareth. John was "the voice of one crying in the wilderness, Make straight the way of the Lord" (John 1:23).

John had bought the truth he preached. He understood that he had to stand with the truth and live it out day by day. Only then would it have an edge sharp enough to cut down any trees.

A lot of people borrow truth. They like to quote certain verses of Scripture when they need something, as if the Bible is a magic book of incantations for conjuring up anything we desire. It isn't. On the contrary, the Bible clearly states that God is not mocked. He cannot be manipulated or controlled, conjured or cajoled. He is Creator and Lord of the universe and the Bible is His book. He inspired it and men wrote it under the guidance of His Spirit. It contains no incantations or artifacts for getting what we want or for chasing away demons. The Bible is not a book of magic spells; it is a book of *truth*.

Power and effectiveness and the "sharp edge" in our lives as Christians come not from merely *hearing* or even *knowing* the truth but from *buying* it for ourselves. I'm not talking about "buying" our way into heaven, but about investing ourselves in the truth to take ownership of it and make it personal for us. Only by taking personal ownership of the truth will it become real and effective in our lives. We must "buy the truth and sell it not."

Owning the Truth Costs Something

Buying implies cost. In order to be the people of truth and live our lives authentically and honestly, we must be willing to pay the price to own the truth. The things in life that mean the most to us and make the biggest difference are the things we have paid for ourselves and therefore claim ownership over. Ownership usually means we have worked hard to acquire or achieve that which we own. If we are not willing to buy the truth, we are probably selling out for something else.

People whose lives are adrift are people who have no truth that they live by. They are like the man Jesus talks about who built his house on the sand only to see the storm and the waves blow it away because it had no foundation (Matt. 7:26-27). Truth is the foundation that anchors our lives. When we stand on truth, nothing can shake us or blow us away—but we have to be willing to pay the price.

Owning the truth means refusing to change or compromise on some things no matter what it costs us: a job, a friendship, a business account, our reputation, or depending on what is at stake, even our lives. History is full of heroes—both men and women—who stood firmly for truth and paid with their lives for that stance. For them, truth was a priceless commodity dearly bought and not for sale at any price.

Contrary to its claims otherwise, the world as a whole opposes truth because truth threatens the predominant culture and power structures, which are founded on lies and deception. As impressive and as formidable as those structures appear, they have no solid foundation. When confronted by the truth they will crumble and be swept away. Error and evil can never stand against truth. They may be able to hide it for a while but they cannot keep it under raps forever. Because God is Truth, truth is a fundamental law of the universe and anything untrue ultimately cannot survive.

Standing in the truth we know and believe, no matter what the cost, gives us ownership of that truth and prepares us to go to the next level in our walk with the Lord. The reason so many Christians live mediocre lives is because when pressure comes they throw out the things they say they believe in return for a compromise that preserves their comfort or their convenience or their status or their pocketbook. Then they wonder why they can never get ahead; why they can never go anywhere with God. They are trying to live on borrowed truth. Until they are willing to invest themselves and buy into the truth they claim to believe, they will never go anywhere.

When we get serious about declaring and standing in the truth, God will provide us with opportunities to buy that truth. In other words, He will set us up in situations where we have to decide whether we will stand up or sell out. Buying the truth means standing up no matter what; selling out is not an option. Once we have stood and endured for the sake of a truth we believe, we will own that truth in a way we never have before. Let's look at some examples.

Shadrach, Meshach and Abednego bought the truth that the God of their fathers was the one true God who alone was to be worshipped. Standing in that truth they defied the king of Babylon saying, "If you throw us in the fiery furnace, our God can deliver us if He chooses, but even if He does not, we will not worship your idol." They had bought the truth and were not going to sell at any price, even if it meant their lives. God brought them safely through the inferno, and on the other side they *owned* the truth in a way they never had before because now they knew what it meant to endure the hardest test in the name of truth.

Daniel bought truth as well when he knowingly defied the king's edict prohibiting prayer to anyone except the king and continued to pray to his God as he always did. His defiance of the king won him a night with the lions but after he survived uneaten and unscathed, he owned the truth that God is faithful.

Paul and Silas were beaten and thrown in jail in Philippi for preaching the gospel. They could have bemoaned their pain and mistreatment and complained to God. Instead, at midnight they were full of joy and singing praises to their Lord. One earthquake later they and all the other prisoners were free but no one escaped. The warden of the jail, however, was saved, along with his entire family. By enduring suffering for the truth, Paul and Silas owned the truth that God is a deliverer, and they saw Him in action again when the jailer and his family were delivered from the darkness of paganism.

Likewise, if we are serious about owning truth, God will put us in situations where we have the opportunity either to "put up or shut up"; perhaps to choose between truth on one side and an enticement that we are reluctant to give up on the other. He does this not to tease us but to test how serious we are because He knows (and wants us to learn) that faith that is acted upon is much stronger than faith that is only spoken about.

The only worship that counts, the only preaching that is powerful, and the only testimony that works, are those that we own; that we have bought with the price of faithfulness against all odds. Until we have paid the price ourselves, we cannot understand the full value of truth. King David, when offered a threshing floor as a gift so he could build an altar to the Lord, insisted on buying it at its full price saying, "Neither will I offer burnt offerings unto the Lord my God of that which doth cost me nothing" (2 Sam. 24:24).

Truth that can change the image and transform our culture is truth that we must be willing to buy and take ownership of no matter what it costs. How we handle truth reveals our character. Martin Luther King, Jr. said that the true measure of a man is not where he stands in days of comfort and convenience but where he stands in days of controversy and trouble. Owning truth carries a cost. There is no such thing as cheap truth.

Let's be willing to pay for what we believe or else let's quit talking about it. Let's stop trying to live on somebody else's revelation or mimic somebody else's relationship. It's time to stop trying to chop trees with a borrowed axe head. Let's buy the truth for ourselves and stand in it, even against the storm, for the storm is where we will *mature* in the truth and learn to *speak* the truth with confidence and authority.

Maturing in the Truth

God will bless us in proportion to our operating in truth. None of us possess all the truth at any given time but if we walk in the truth that we have and in the light that we see; if we proceed faithfully to do what we know is right in the understanding that we possess, God will bless us proportionately. The more faithful we are with the truth we own, the more blessings He will pour out.

The flip side of the coin is that Satan will curse us in proportion to the truth we reject. Proverbs 3:33 says, "The curse of the Lord is in the house of the wicked: but he blesseth the habitation of the just." There's a big difference between ignorance of the truth and rejection of the truth. In our American legal system ignorance of the law is no excuse. Nevertheless, a person who violates the law in ignorance often receives lighter punishment than someone who deliberately and knowingly breaks the law.

People who are ignorant of the truth of the gospel are held in bondage and spiritual blindness by Satan. Those who know the truth and reject it, however, open themselves up to being cursed. This is true also for Christians. Rejecting the truth may be as simple as failing to walk in a truth that has been revealed to us. Another word for this is disobedience. Truth rejection doesn't mean we will lose our salvation but it does mean that we open ourselves up to curses and satanic harassment in proportion to the truth we reject.

Jesus said, "If ye continue in my word, then are ye my disciples indeed; And ye shall know the truth, and the truth shall make you free" (John 8:31-32). Freedom comes from walking in the truth. The opposite should be obvious: failure to walk in the truth results in bondage. Our freedom over Satan's influence in our lives does not depend on how many spiritual warfare conferences we attend or how many different ways we learn to "bind" him, but on how committed we are to knowing, owning and walking in the truth.

In His high-priestly prayer the night before His crucifixion, Jesus prayed for His disciples, saying, "Sanctify them through thy truth: thy word is truth" (John 17:17). Sanctification has to do with maturity. It refers to the process of growing in the likeness of Christ. This verse reveals that, just as walking in the truth brings us freedom, it also matures us in our faith.

Just as in our natural life, our spiritual life progresses from infancy to maturity. As a loving Father, God imparts to all of us a measure of grace to cover us in our ignorance, not to bless our ignorance but to protect us as He walks us into greater and greater knowledge of the truth.

Truth is the primary agent that He uses to mature us. For example, God will never lie to us to make us better. When God speaks, He always speaks truth. Because God *is* truth it can be no other way. In the same way, Jesus always speaks the truth. He will be silent rather than lie.

God also reveals truth to us according to our maturity level. Jesus once told His disciples, "I have yet many things to say unto you, but ye cannot bear them now. Howbeit when he, the Spirit of truth, is come, he will guide you into all truth" (John 16:12-13a). Jesus always speaks truth but never beyond our capacity to receive it. The Holy Spirit guides us into greater knowledge as we are ready.

Have you ever been truthful to someone beyond his or her ability to handle it and discovered you did more harm than good? Truth is powerful; it can devastate the unprepared. In our zeal to do the right thing we may pledge to be "completely truthful" without considering the effect that might have on others. The Bible tells us to speak the truth in love (Eph. 4:15) but just because we love somebody doesn't give us the right to say everything we want to say at any time. And just because something is true doesn't give us the right to say it if we can't say it in love. Sometimes the wiser course is to chop the truth up into smaller, bite-sized pieces that are easier to digest. The other recourse is to remain silent until a better opportunity comes. Lying is never an option.

Maturity, then, can be defined at least partially as the measure of our ability to receive truth. Perhaps one of the highest levels of maturity is the ability to receive truth against self interest. Martin Luther King, Jr. used to say that one of the greatest definitions of maturity is the ability to be self-critical; to be able to look at oneself critically and see our own faults and be introspective. These are the kind of people we honor, people who will receive truth even after they have staked an opposing position but have come to realize they are wrong. Saying, "I was wrong," is almost as hard as saying, "I'm sorry." Both statements require a great deal of maturity. A mature person will always side with truth, even if doing so requires switching sides, because he understands that truth will set him free.

All of us know someone in our life we admire because they loved us enough to tell us the truth even at the risk of offending us because they were so committed to our growth and maturity. They knew us well enough to know that we would get over it. Those are the kind of people who help us grow; people who love us enough not to leave us in error or coddle us in sin but to tell us the truth even when it is painful. Who are the teachers we remember and respect the most in later years? Those who required the most out of us. It's human nature. In spite of our complaining and whining, deep down inside, we want to be challenged; we want to be prodded and motivated and encouraged to move beyond our comfort zone and become all we can be.

We live in a culture that desperately needs to hear the truth, even if it's painful. As Christians, we possess the truth our culture needs to hear. The truth of God must become an invading force into every area of our lives in all of our ways so that it can spill out into the world around us. One of the ways that God wants to project His truth into the culture is through the witness and ministry of the Church. Christ never intended for His Church to be a purely social institution for the gathering of social misfits. Throughout the ages the Church has stood as a prophetic voice proclaiming truth to the people of every generation. Maturity in Christ—maturity in the truth—prepares us to speak that truth to our generation with confidence and authority.

Speaking the Truth

Ownership of the truth gives us the courage and boldness to speak the truth when needed because we have paid the price for it—we have "gone through the fire" so to speak. Truth is no longer just theory for us but a dynamic, living reality. Many churches speak the truth in the sense of proclaiming a message that is theologically and doctrinally accurate, but lacking conviction because they have never been tested. They may believe the gospel to be true but it still remains in large measure theory for them. Churches preaching and teaching theory will never change the world.

A culture in crisis needs a church that is not afraid to speak the truth with the fire of conviction and the confidence of divine authority. Such boldness arises when we are secure in the knowledge of our assignment and in the reality of Christ's presence with us to carry it out. Jesus said, "All power is given unto me in heaven and in earth. Go ye therefore, and teach all nations, baptizing them in the name of the Father, and of the Son, and of the Holy Ghost: Teaching them to observe all things whatsoever I have commanded you: and, lo, I am with you alway, even unto the end of the world" (Matt. 28:18-20). Jesus has commissioned us to speak truth to the nations and promised His continuing and sustaining presence to enable us to do it.

Speaking the truth will be at times just as costly as buying it because even though the world needs to hear the truth, the world does not want to hear the truth. God's truth exposes the lies and deception that are the foundation for the world's social and cultural systems. The powers of darkness that lie behind those systems respond vigorously and sometimes violently against such exposure. This is why Jesus cautioned His followers:

18If the world hate you, ye know that it hated me before it hated you. 19If ye were of the world, the world would love his own: but because ye are not of the world, but I have chosen you out of the world, therefore the world hateth you. 20Remember the word that I said unto you, The servant is not greater than his lord. If they have persecuted me, they will also persecute you; if they have kept my saying, they will keep yours also (John 15:18-20).

Speaking to Nicodemus, Jesus said:

19And this is the condemnation, that light is come into the world, and men loved darkness rather than light, because their deeds were evil. 20For every one that doeth evil hateth the light, neither cometh to the light, lest his deeds should be reproved. 21But he that doeth truth cometh to the light, that his deeds may be made manifest, that they are wrought in God (John 3:19-21).

The powers of darkness that control the cultural, social, and religious systems of the world hate the things of God, the ways of God, and the people of God and respond to them with implacable hostility. This is why churches and individual Christians who become serious about living for Christ and speaking the truth always face so much resistance. The fight may be long and it may be hard, but ultimately the victory is ours because Christ has made us "more than conquerors" (Rom. 8:37) and because "greater is he that is in [us] than he that is in the world" (1 John 4:4).

Despite the fact that the world system as a whole remains hostile toward biblical truth and the gospel, we nevertheless live in a day of unprecedented opportunity for the Church to advance in changing the image and impacting our culture for

Christ. Interest in spirituality in general has risen in recent years to the point where perhaps more people than ever before are at least open to some kind of spiritual dimension to their lives. Disillusionment with the failed utopian promises of science and technology as well as the purposelessness of life without a moral anchor has prompted more and more people to turn to some form of spirituality for answers.

Amidst the multitude of voices and philosophies clamoring for the attention of men, the voice of the Church should be the loudest and the clearest because out of all those voices we alone possess the truth. And what is the truth? The truth is that "God was in Christ, reconciling the world unto himself, not imputing their trespasses unto them; and hath committed unto us the word of reconciliation" (2 Cor. 5:19).

This is the truth that we must own and speak to our day and our generation. This is the truth that can change the image and has the power to transform our culture. This is the truth that will shift power from the forces of darkness and the institutions and philosophies they undergird to the people of God and the cause of righteousness. This is the truth that is coming to the fore in conjunction with the emerging *apostolic generation*.

Gathering

There are at least six practical ways that the Church can confront the dominant culture with the aim of changing the climate. The first way is through *gathering*.

One of the most effective ways to influence our culture and bring expression to the Spirit of God in time and space is by the simple act of gathering together. When we gather as the body of Christ, we come together in agreement as one people of one heart and one mind. As individuals, we are all different, with different thoughts, different backgrounds, different experiences, different gifts and talents, and different interests. Gathering together as one body of Christ unites us with a common vision, a common purpose, and a common goal. We remain individuals with our own independent thoughts and feelings, but those differences are subordinated to the common oneness we share as a family of God in Christ.

It is for the sake of this essential unity that the Bible tells us to gather together regularly:

> *23Let us hold fast the profession of our faith without wavering; (for he is faithful that promised;) 24And let us consider one another to provoke unto love and to good works: 25Not forsaking the assembling of ourselves together, as the manner of some is; but exhorting one another: and so much the more, as ye see the day approaching* (Hebrews 10:23-25).

Gathering together helps us "hold fast" our profession of faith "without wavering." We draw courage and encouragement from each other, both in standing firm in our faith and in motivating each other to "love and to good works."

One of the greatest challenges the Church faces in this new millennium is the danger of separation and fragmentation. More than ever before, media such as radio, television and, especially, the internet, make it easy for believers to become "Lone Ranger Christians." Why go to the trouble of getting up and going to church when we can turn on the television or the radio or log on to the internet and find a church service to watch and a preacher to listen to?

Don't get me wrong; modern media, including the internet, are valuable tools that we should use readily to help get our message out, but they are no substitute for consistent, regular, gathering together as a body of believers. Not only does gathering bring us as independent individuals into common agreement and purpose, but it is also a physical and very compelling demonstration of unity that a desperately fragmented world needs to see.

Worship

A second way the Church influences culture is through *worship*. Worship is our response to the Holy Spirit by exalting God above every other principality or power in heaven or in earth.

When we sing and shout and dance and say "Amen!" and lift up our hands in praise and worship, we become instruments through whom the Holy Spirit finds expression in time and space. Through our worship, that which is invisible—the Spirit of God—becomes visible in us.

Our worship exalts God in the face of a culture and a spirit that says, "We will not serve God." Worship is our way of proclaiming that we will not buckle under to a culture that denies and defies God. We will not be in bondage to its strongholds or live under its climate. Rather, we will live as a counterculture that exalts and acknowledges the living God as Lord of heaven and earth.

When we worship, we give visible testimony to the world that there is another culture—a Kingdom or Dominion culture—that has greater legitimacy than the devil's culture. In worship, we respond to the Spirit of God by declaring that He is over every principality, every power, every might, every dominion, and every name that is named. When the Church of the Lord Jesus Christ comes together in worship, we show a God-denying culture not only that He is real, but also that He rules as sovereign God and is worthy of all our praise and devotion.

Giving

Another way the Church establishes and responds to the Holy Spirit is through *giving*. Giving establishes God as our source. That fact alone sets us against the predominant culture of the day, which says that the Gross National Product is our source, or the government is our source, or our job is our source. When we give our tithes and offerings, we recognize that God is the owner of all things, and we are simply returning to Him a portion of what He has already given us. Learning to give teaches us to keep our possessions and our priorities in proper perspective.

Not only does giving establish God as our source; it also empowers His Kingdom in a practical way. Because of the principles of multiplication and return, whatever we give to God He multiplies exponentially and returns a thousand-fold to advance His Kingdom in ways we could never imagine and could never hope to do on our own.

Giving also helps guard us against greed. God has designed His system in such a way as to bless us without our ever being captured by the spirit of greed. As God blesses us financially, we return the first ten percent to Him and then give something more on top of that in accordance to how He has blessed us. Developing this habit and attitude of the mind breaks the spirit of greed and protects us from the curse of an ungrateful heart.

One of the ways we can respond to a spirit is by demonstrating the same nature as that spirit. God is a giver by nature and a blesser by nature. When we activate ourselves in these same areas, we respond to the Spirit of God and strongholds begin to fall.

Intercession

A fourth way that the Church influences culture and responds to the Holy Spirit, giving Him expression in time and space is through *intercession*.

Intercession undermines the authority of the ruling spirits by weakening their hold on the minds of people. It creates a hedge around those for whom we pray. Intercession releases angelic assistance. It disrupts the demonic atmosphere and opens the windows of heaven for God's Word.

Intercessory prayer helps tear down strongholds. Most Christians know very little about intercessory prayer. Their prayers tend to focus on petition—asking for things for themselves or others. This is fine in its place, but petitionary prayer alone will never change the culture. Culture change calls for intercessory prayer, in which we pray with the purpose of disrupting the spiritual principalities and powers over a region.

Like missiles cutting through enemy territory, we need to pray continually for God's Word to go forth unhindered into every highway and every hedge so that the enemy will not have his way any longer and the Spirit of God will regain authority over a region and bring down the principalities and powers of darkness.

Forgiveness

Another way we respond to the Holy Spirit and influence the culture is by tearing down strongholds through the ministry of *forgiveness*. Jesus said: "Whosoever sins ye remit, they are remitted unto them; and whosoever sins ye retain they are retained" (John 20:23). Part of the ministry that Jesus gave us was the ministry of releasing people from their sin through forgiveness. Forgiveness is the releasing from judgment of saint and sinner alike. It is purposely flowing in unity.

Stated another way, forgiveness means that we don't hold people's sins against them, no matter who they are or what they've done. Our natural response when hurt or offended is to take offense and hold a grudge. We want to get even or hold the offender in bonds of obligation to us. Forgiveness means releasing the offender completely from any obligation to us either in our mind or in theirs.

No kingdom divided against itself can stand. That is why Satan seeks to "divide and conquer" by sowing seeds of offense and unforgiveness in the Church. As long as we hold people to an offense, we are living in the culture of the world, and when we live in the culture of the world, we build a stronghold in the Church!

Forgiveness promotes and preserves unity, and when the Church is united and unified, not even the gates of hell can stand against us!

Ministry Mantles

Finally, we respond to the Holy Spirit, tear down strongholds, and influence culture by understanding and utilizing *ministry mantles*. This involves flowing under the directives of God's appointed leadership, moving through delegated authority to strategically assault enemy-held territory.

God appoints and anoints, calls and commissions, and authorizes and deputizes certain people for specific ministries. He places certain anointings, or ministry mantles, on their lives. With this measure of authority, they relate and submit to those with greater authority, and operate under the direction of appointed leadership.

In this way we begin to move strategically rather than haphazardly, with deliberation and purpose rather than chaotically, and as a unified body rather than a disorganized mob. Moving in a ministry mantle under delegated authority gives us the covering and enabling we need to tear down the strongholds of the enemy. When we function under that mantle, we are functioning under the directive of God-given leadership. Therefore, we carry with that mantle the commissioning and the authority of that headship ministry that has commissioned us and released us to go.

Purposely and strategically we move in and take a brick out of the stronghold here, and then another brick over there. We keep pushing and interceding and lifting Jesus higher and higher. We keep pulling and gathering and giving and worshipping and praying and forgiving and releasing one person from bondage and then another, and another. One person gets healed and another person gets saved. Praise goes up and another gathering happens until it all begins to overflow. This process repeats until eventually, the stronghold has to come down!

We must remember the words of Romans 12:21: "Be not overcome of evil, but overcome evil with good." We must believe the Word of God that light is stronger than darkness, order is stronger than chaos, love is stronger than hate, blessing is stronger than cursing, forgiveness is stronger than unforgiveness, and unity is stronger than division.

We must take all these things to heart and become a counterculture in the midst of the world: a walking billboard, a sign and a wonder, the physical and ultimate expression of an invisible, eternal kingdom manifest in time and space in the material, physical, and temporary world. We are the Church, and our calling from Christ, our Head, is to carry His message to the north, south, east and west, tearing down strongholds wherever we go and changing the spiritual climate all over the world!

Power and influence are not permanent nor are they static. They are fluid and dynamic. Power moves.

"For riches are not for ever: and doth the crown endure to every generation?"
— Proverbs 27:24

Chapter Three

Changing the Climate

The time has come for the Church to stand up in faith, power, and authority and tell the devil that he is about to be evicted!

As the corporate body of Christ, our calling is to make disciples in every nation, setting them free from the bondage of sin and Satan's deceptions and breaking his strongholds in their minds. We are called to change the climate. This is a task that requires all of us working together as God's people in harmony of vision and purpose. It requires a corporate body and a corporate anointing.

When Jesus was here on the earth, He accomplished this by Himself because in Him dwelled "the fullness of the Godhead bodily" (Col. 2:9). This is a divine mystery that we cannot explain or even fully understand. The fullness of God was present in the physical body of Jesus. Whatever the Father in heaven desired, Jesus carried out on earth.

It is different with us. Even though as Christians we carry the image and likeness of God and His Spirit dwells within us, the fullness of God does not reside in us. That was unique to Jesus. We have power and authority, but not at the level Jesus did. He is the Head, we are the body. The body does what the Head commands. First Corinthians 12:27 says that we are the corporate "body of Christ" on earth, and each one of us "members in particular." What Jesus did by Himself now takes His body working together to do.

Changing the climate requires a body of Christ that collectively understands not only the power, authority, and anointing we possess to tear down strongholds and displace demonic forces, but also our role as agents for bringing in a great harvest of souls for the Kingdom of God. We need to be confident that the harvest is ours. God says in Psalm 2:8, "Ask of me, and I shall give thee the heathen for thine inheritance, and the uttermost parts of the earth for thy possession." The earth is the Lord's, and He has given it to His children—us. The devil is a trespasser and a usurper who has no right or claim to the earth or anything or anyone on it. He has no right to us, our families, or our things; no right to our cities or our nations. He is but a pretender to the throne who has already been judged and sentenced and awaits God's timing for his final destruction.

In the meantime, he struts around and acts tough and works ceaselessly to deceive people into believing that he is still in charge. It is our job as the corporate body of Christ to stand up and serve notice to the enemy that by the finger of God he is cast out and the Kingdom of God has come in.

In ancient times, when kingdoms went to war, the attacking king dispatched messengers bearing his insignia on banners and flags. These messengers would enter the capital city of the opposing king, plant their flags, and declare, "Give up or be conquered!" The only thing the devil understands is greater force. He will give in only when one more powerful than he comes against him. As the corporate body of Christ, what we do through praise and worship, through preaching and prophesying, and through collective agreement, is run into the devil's territory, plant the flag of our King, and say to Satan, "Give up or be conquered!" We come not in our own name or in our own power but in the name and power of the King of kings who sends us and commissions us.

Changing the climate and displacing the powers of darkness have nothing to do with our ability but, rather, His ability working through us. By ourselves, we will never be able to bring the harvest in. Only by working in conjunction with the Spirit of God will we see strongholds topple and the spiritual climate change over our cities and nations. Remember the words of Zechariah 4:6: "Not by might, nor by power, but by my spirit, saith the Lord of hosts."

When we as a corporate body of Christ begin functioning in agreement with His Spirit, we have the capacity to change the spiritual climate of a region. We can stamp that area with such holy intensity that people begin to be drawn to the Spirit of God. All we have to do is lift Jesus up boldly and consistently in everything we do; the Holy Spirit will do the drawing. Jesus said: "And I, if I be lifted up from the earth, will draw all men unto me" (John 12:32).

No More Backing Up

Before we can successfully stand up to Satan and engage him on his own turf, we have to reach the place in our individual and collective hearts where we say, "Enough is enough!" At some point in life, every one of us will face something that challenges everything we believe at one moment, and we will have to decide where we stand. The thing itself may appear incidental, yet it somehow represents to us everything we believe. There will come a time when we have backed up as far as we are willing to back up and we have no option left but to stand and fight. Some things we can concede and give in on without sacrificing our beliefs or integrity. Some things are negotiable; others are not. People or circumstances can back us into a corner to the point where we dig in our heels and refuse to give up any more ground. It's either fight or die, and we choose to fight because everything we love and believe in is on the line. We've reached the point of no return, the straw that breaks the camel's back. In the immortal words of Popeye the Sailor, "That's all I can stands, 'cause I can't stands no more!"

Fiddler on the Roof, the hit Broadway musical, tells the story of Tevye, a Russian Jewish milkman of a century ago who must deal with his daughters' breaks with tradition. As each daughter makes a decision that goes against custom and the ways of their tiny village, Tevye debates within himself about their choices: "On the one hand…On the other hand." In this way he reconciles himself with their decisions and with the changing times that brought them about.

Tevye's method succeeds—until his youngest daughter runs off and marries a Gentile. Tortured in heart, Tevye nevertheless tries to reconcile with this latest turn of events. He is unsuccessful, saying at one point, "If I bend that far I'll break." Finally, his face set in grim resolution, he declares, "On the other hand…there *is* no other hand!" Tevye has backed up as far as he can go. He has conceded all the ground he can concede. He can't give in any further without sacrificing everything he believes as a Jew.

The Bible relates the story of another Jew, Shammah, who reached the point where he had backed up all he could and said, "No more!" Shammah was one of the "mighty men," thirty incomparable warriors who were part of King David's inner circle. His story is found in the 23rd chapter of Second Samuel as part of a listing of the "mighty men" and their deeds of valor:

And after him was Shammah the son of Agee the Hararite. And the Philistines were gathered together into a troop, where was a piece of ground full of lentils: and the people fled from the Philistines. But he stood in the midst of the ground, and defended it, and slew the Philistines: and the Lord wrought a great victory (2 Samuel 23:11-12).

For centuries the Philistines had been a thorn in Israel's side. Many times their raiding parties had attacked the Israelites during harvest season, stealing all their grain or fruit or other crops, leaving the Israelites with no harvest. On this occasion, however, it was different. When a "troop" of Philistines descended on a certain lentil patch with scavenging in mind, all the Israelites there fled in fear—all except Shammah. This "mighty man" did *not* flee. Scripture says that Shammah "stood in the midst of the ground, and defended it." Shammah dug in his heels, faced the Philistines and said, "No way. Not today. You picked on the wrong guy. I'm not backing up anymore. You want a piece of me? Come get it, if you can! Who wants to be first?"

For Shammah, there was more to this than simply defending a lentil patch—a lot more. It was about standing firm against an enemy that hated him and his people (the people of God) and opposed everything they believed in and held dear. Perhaps these particular Philistines were hungry and simply wanted to increase their supply of lentils. That was beside the point. As far as Shammah was concerned, this was a life or death issue. It was fight or flight, sink or swim, put up or shut up. The Philistines had raided once too often and Shammah stood fast and said, "No more!"

It was a *watershed moment.* When Shammah stood his ground against the enemy, he brought himself into agreement with a greater power: the power of God who said: "I've never wanted them to take that from you." Because he was in agreement with God, Shammah was able to stand in that lentil patch and single-handedly kill every Philistine that came against him. It was a partnership effort. Shammah did the work but he was not alone, for the Scripture says that "the Lord wrought a great victory." What was the key to Shammah's success? Getting into agreement with God. And that didn't happen until Shammah reached the point of realizing that he had no more backing up left in him.

Watershed Moments

Shammah's firm stance in that lentil patch was a watershed moment, an event that shaped the character and climate of everything that followed. Every society has watershed moments where events transpire that release and activate something to shift in the spirit. As we have already seen, Woodstock is one example. How can we account for the phenomenon of Woodstock? The seminal rock music festival of the 20th century was plagued by confusion over the location, bad advertising, and torrential rains, yet in the summer of 1969 nearly half a million young Americans camped out in the rain and mud for three days of music, drugs, and the celebration of the "flower power" generation. It was almost like a supernatural draw; people came from all over the country. Then the popular psalmists and minstrels of the day got up and began to release their spirit into an entire generation of young people.

The American civil rights movement provided many watershed moments that changed the course of history in our country. What about the landmark Supreme Court case *Brown v. Board of Education* where NAACP attorney (and later U.S. Supreme Court Justice) Thurgood Marshall declared that "separate but equal" as a justification for segregation in public schools was a fallacy and that separate was inherently unequal? Or how about the National March on Washington in 1963 that evidenced a growing level of white support for civil rights? What about Rosa Park's refusal to give up her bus seat to a white man and whose subsequent arrest sparked a massive boycott by African-Americans of the city buses in Birmingham, Alabama?

All of these were watershed moments that profoundly shaped the future. So was the 1973 U.S. Supreme Court decision *Roe v. Wade*. Who today would not agree that this decision legalizing abortion in the United States has profoundly affected the spirit and character of American society and culture over the past thirty years? Overnight our country went from having some of the most restrictive abortion laws in the world to some of the most liberalized. Almost nowhere else in the world is it as easy for a woman to get an abortion as it is in the United States. According to some estimates, upwards of 50,000,000 legal abortions have been performed in America since 1973. Fifty million unborn children killed in the womb, a number equivalent to nearly one-fifth of America's population.

Was *Roe v. Wade* a watershed moment for America? Without a doubt. Watershed moments are not always positive; sometimes they are destructive to a people's moral or spiritual health. The 1962 *Engel v. Vitale* decision by the U.S. Supreme Court determined that prayer in public schools violated the First Amendment's prohibition against the establishment of religion. *Murray v. Curlett*, the following year, reached the same conclusion regarding Bible reading in the public schools.

The Boston Tea Party of 1773 was a watershed moment that helped lay the groundwork for the American Revolution. A band of working men from Boston, disguised as Mohawk Indians, boarded ships recently arrived from England and threw overboard 342 chests of tea in protest of oppressive and unfair taxes imposed on the colonies by Parliament. So the real issue was not tea but what the tea represented: taxation without representation. By destroying the cargo of tea, the protesters were taking a stand on an issue they held to be nonnegotiable. Their actions were their way of saying, "Enough is enough! No more backing up!"

I believe that God is waiting for some of His people to reach the same point. He is waiting for those who will stand up and say to the enemy, "Enough is enough! You've taken prayer and Bible reading out of our schools. You've killed millions of our unborn babies. You've attacked our homes, our families, and even the institution of marriage itself. We've watched it happen and it's gone on long enough. That's it! It's over! No more backing up! We're going to preach the gospel and stand firm for the truth. We're going to walk in obedience to Christ. By the power of God, we're going to take you on and we're going to take you out!"

Reaching Beyond the Walls

The people who have the most lasting impact on society and culture are those who are able to transcend type; who are able to reach beyond their own immediate circle of like-minded folks and bring into it people who were initially opposed to them or their ideas. Not satisfied just to "preach to the choir," these individuals set out to cast a large net to draw folks of many different persuasions into one common cause. This is the only way to have a wide-ranging influence on the greater culture. Unless we can reach out to those who are unlike us and who disagree with us and win them over, all we will have is our own little homogeneous group, a subculture with little lasting influence.

One such transcendent individual was the late Dr. Martin Luther King, Jr. Dr. King was neither the first nor the last person to speak about civil rights, but he spoke in such a way as to transcend race, religion, and politics, winning over to his cause many people, including many whites, who at first opposed both him and the goals of the civil rights movement. Although he has been dead for nearly forty years, Dr. King's legacy lives on. Our society is vastly different today than it would have been without his influence.

Louis Armstrong, the legendary jazz trumpeter, transcended his immediate musical circle, becoming recognized during his lifetime as one of America's foremost unofficial "good will ambassadors." Even people who knew nothing about jazz music were drawn to his infectious personality and love of life.

And what about Elvis Presley and Johnny Cash? The influence of these two giants on the overall music industry could hardly be overestimated. As musicians they are hard to classify, and even during their lifetimes they were acknowledged as major inspirations for an entire generation of musical performers. Even now, many of today's up-and-coming musicians cite Presley and Cash as major influences on their own music. Elvis Presley and Johnny Cash were and remain transcendent individuals.

My point is this: if we want to change the climate and influence our culture for Christ, we have to be able to reach beyond the confines of our own like-minded group. We must step outside the four walls of our church and engage in meaningful dialogue with people who are outside our circle of belief and draw them in.

It seems that in so many of our churches, we spend most of our time trying to fortify the few people who agree with us. There are many church folks who are unclear about what they believe and why. Some don't understand the purpose and importance of praise and worship, while others do not tithe because they are not yet convinced that God is truly a trustworthy Provider who will care for all their needs. Still others either do not know or do not trust the teachings of Jesus concerning such matters as mercy and forgiveness enough to practice them in their lives on any consistent basis.

Building up and edifying fellow believers is indeed an important part of the Church's ministry, but that alone will not change the spiritual climate. Impacting our culture for Christ requires an aggressive evangelism that focuses on drawing into belief in the gospel message those who currently are opposed to it. In other words, God wants us to transcend. He wants us to outgrow our labels of Pentecostal or Charismatic or Baptist or Catholic or whatever. How we label ourselves is not as important as the message we proclaim. The important issue is being so in agreement with heaven that we transcend our own ethnicity, our own city, our own stronghold, our own past, and our own hurt and thus draw to the Kingdom of God those who would never have come had we not stood and done something.

Dealing with Levels of Demonic Influence

Before we engage the enemy on any kind of systematic basis to bring down strongholds and change the climate, it is important that we understand not only the different levels of demonic influence, but also the levels of authority that we have for dealing with them.

The most basic level is one-on-one demonic influence: the demonization of individuals. Many people are bound up in some way or another and don't know how to get free. They do things they don't want to do and cannot understand why they keep doing them. In many cases they seem to be caught up in patterns of poverty, failure, self-destructive behavior, depression, or other types of dysfunction. While these patterns do not *automatically* mean that someone is demon-possessed, they are warning signs that could indicate possible demonic influence. Careful discernment is necessary to determine which is which.

Every born-again, Spirit-filled Christian possesses the power and authority from God to deal with unclean spirits on a one-to-one individual basis. Greater is He that is in us than he that is in the world. Casting out a demon does not require holy water. It doesn't call for a cross or a big Bible, or any other kind of religious paraphernalia. All it requires of us is a humble spirit that recognizes the power and authority the Lord has delegated to us and acknowledges our total dependence on Him.

The Lord has deputized, authorized, appointed and anointed us to deal with demonic influence on an individual basis. We cannot deliver someone who does not want to be delivered, but we can help those who ask for it. By the authority vested in us by Christ, *and in His Name*, we can command an unclean spirit to depart, and it will leave. It has no choice. The power is not in us but in the Name of the One we represent.

At the next level lies what the Bible refers to as "doctrines of devils," which is part of what is involved with discerning the times. Paul, writing to Timothy, said, "Now the Spirit speaketh expressly, that in the latter times some shall depart from the faith, giving heed to seducing spirits, and doctrines of devils" (1 Tim. 4:1). Simply stated, doctrines of devils are demonically-inspired doctrines, teachings and ideas that seek to gain strongholds in the minds of men. This level of demonic influence goes beyond an individual basis to become a theology, a philosophy, a world-view, a collective consciousness, an ascribed-to pattern, a dogma; a way of thinking that people adopt that facilitates them in their bondage.

Although we as individual Christians have authority over demons on a one-to-one basis, we cannot deal with doctrines of devils by ourselves. Doctrines of devils must be attacked, not simply cast out. This is one reason, among others, why Christ gave to His Church the five-fold ministry of apostles, prophets, pastors, evangelists and teachers. Part of the purpose of the five-fold ministry is to attack doctrines of devils, to tear down the strongholds of demonically inspired lies and deceptions in the minds of people and replace them with biblical truth. Knowledge of the truth brings freedom from bondage, Jesus said, "Ye shall know the truth, and the truth shall make you free" (John 8:32).

The highest level of demonic influence is the level of governing spirits or principalities and powers that affect climates. The climate has to be right for a doctrine of devils to succeed. For example, Adolf Hitler was able to rise to power in Germany and enact his demonically-inspired policies because a climate was established that paved the way. The German people, humiliated by their defeat in World War One and their subsequent treatment by the victorious Allies, and hungry and destitute because of the Great Depression and the failure of Germany's economy, were ripe to respond to Hitler's promise to restore their pride, dignity, honor, prosperity, and greatness as a people. The climate of anger, humiliation and despair provided fertile soil for Hitler's devilish doctrines to take root.

Such a negative spiritual climate does not arise by itself. The enemy works on the climate until people are ready to hear something that will ensnare them in a particular way.

Individual Christians can cast out demons on a one-to-one basis. The five-fold ministry can attack and supplant doctrines of devils with biblical truth. But the only way to dislodge an entrenched demonic principality is for the people of God to come together in unity and in agreement with each other and with God. Jesus promised, "If two of you shall agree on earth as touching any thing that they shall ask, it shall be done for them of my Father which is in heaven. For where two or three are gathered together in my name, there am I in the midst of them" (Matt. 18:19-20).

As the Church, we are called *together* to rise up into the high places and do battle with principalities and powers and cast down every imagination and every high thing that exalts itself against the knowledge of God. That is our calling and our destiny. The key is to get into *agreement* with God.

Agreeing with God

Getting into agreement with God is crucial for changing the spiritual climate because our conflict is not with flesh and blood but with spiritual principalities and powers of the air. That kind of adversary cannot be defeated with physical weapons or resources. We are engaged in a life-or-death spiritual war, and the first thing we need to remember is that *the battle is always won or lost in the spirit before it ever hits the earth.* That is why we need to get ourselves into agreement with God before we start.

No matter what the issue, we win or lose our battles in our mind long before they ever become physical. Show me someone who has a defeated attitude and I'll show you someone who is going to lose, regardless of the problem. On the other hand, show me a person who has a victorious attitude and I'll show you a person who is going to win regardless of the odds or the obstacles.

It is because our battles are won or lost in the spirit first that we must be spiritual people. Our natural minds do not comprehend or discern the things of the Spirit of God. To understand spiritual things we must become spiritually-minded. We don't always understand how a natural action produces a spiritual result, but it has to do with agreeing with what heaven has already said.

Agreeing with the things of God will automatically put us at odds with the prevailing spirits and viewpoints. Just look at

Jesus. He was the most controversial man of His day, and not just occasionally. Jesus was pervasively, continually, and purposely controversial. Why? Because He did the works of His Father, which put Him at odds with the prevailing powers.

Jesus said that part of the purpose of the Kingdom of God is to displace principalities and powers at all levels. This is what He Himself did. He cast demons out of individuals, taught correctives to the doctrines of devils that pervaded His society ("Ye have heard that it was said…But I say unto you…"), and even dealt with governing and ruling spirits.

He put His Spirit within us so that we could be in agreement with Him. Therefore, all of God's people, whoever and wherever we may be, need to take a certain degree of ownership in our own territory. We cannot by ourselves change every place, nor has God called us to do so. He has people in other places as well for that very purpose. Our responsibility is to put our feet down where we are and say: "This is our city," or "This is our county," or "This is our state." Why? Because that is where God has put us.

God has planted us where we are so that we can announce that the Kingdom of God has come to our region. It's time for the captives to be set free; for the junkies and the alcoholics to be delivered from their addictions. It's time for the young men to be renewed and strengthened and purified in their minds and for the young women to regain their self-respect and self-value. It's time for our families to be healed and made whole again and for the devil to let go of our finances. It's time to trade our tears of sorrow for the "oil of gladness" (Ps. 45:7) and the "spirit of heaviness" for the "garment of praise" (Isa. 61:3).

It's time to get in agreement with God and announce that the Kingdom of heaven is here and that the harvest is now. We can proclaim this boldly because in the spirit it's already done!

"The Battle Is Not Yours, but God's"

The Old Testament is full of examples of how battles are won in the spirit as soon as God's people come into agreement with Him. Consider the experience of Jehoshaphat, one of the few truly godly and righteous kings of Judah. When a great army of Moabites and Ammonites came against him, Jehoshaphat turned to the Lord and proclaimed a fast throughout the kingdom. Standing before the people in the Temple, Jehoshaphat appealed to the Lord. After praising God and acknowledging Him as the One who brought them into the land, the king prayed for God's intervention in their current circumstances:

> *¹⁰And now, behold, the children of Ammon and Moab and mount Seir, whom thou wouldest not let Israel invade, when they came out of the land of Egypt, but they turned from them, and destroyed them not; ¹¹Behold, I say, how they reward us, to come to cast us out of thy possession, which thou hast given us to inherit. ¹²O our God, wilt thou not judge them? for we have no might against this great company that cometh against us; neither know we what to do: but our eyes are upon thee* (2 Chronicles 20:10-12).

Jehoshaphat cast himself and his people into the capable hands of God, saying, "We're not strong enough to fight this enemy, and we don't know what to do, but we're looking to You for help. With this attitude of faith and surrender, Jehoshaphat came into agreement with God, and God's answer was swift. The Spirit of the Lord came upon a man named Jahaziel, who spoke the Lord's answer to the king:

15And he said, Hearken ye, all Judah, and ye inhabitants of Jerusalem, and thou king Jehoshaphat, Thus saith the Lord unto you, Be not afraid nor dismayed by reason of this great multitude; for the battle is not yours, but God's. 16To morrow go ye down against them: behold, they come up by the cliff of Ziz; and ye shall find them at the end of the brook, before the wilderness of Jeruel. 17Ye shall not need to fight in this battle: set yourselves, stand ye still, and see the salvation of the Lord with you, O Judah and Jerusalem: fear not, nor be dismayed; to morrow go out against them: for the Lord will be with you (2 Chronicles 20:15-17).

When the king and the people came into agreement with God, the Lord said, "The battle is not yours, but God's." In other words, God was going to fight for them. The strategy they employed was unique for a military campaign. As the army marched out for battle, Jehoshaphat placed singers in front who went forth singing and praising God. In the end, the enemy was completely destroyed, and Jehoshaphat's army never had to lift a finger:

22And when they began to sing and to praise, the Lord set ambushments against the children of Ammon, Moab, and mount Seir, which were come against Judah; and they were smitten. 23For the children of Ammon and Moab stood up against the inhabitants of mount Seir, utterly to slay and destroy them: and when they had made an end of the inhabitants of Seir, every one helped to destroy another (2 Chronicles 20:22-23).

As soon as Jehoshaphat's singers began praising God, He set the Moabites and Ammonites against the inhabitants of mount Seir, and then against each other until they completely destroyed each other. The battle was won in the spirit when Jehoshaphat and the people came into agreement with God, and God brought the victory.

The Sword of the Lord and of Gideon

Gideon is another Old Testament figure who discovered the power of being in agreement with God. One day Gideon was threshing wheat in a winepress to hide his activities from the Midianites, who raided Israel frequently and stole their grain and other crops. The angel of the Lord appeared to Gideon and said, "The Lord is with thee, thou mighty man of valor…Go in this thy might, and thou shalt save Israel from the hand of the Midianites: have not I sent thee?" (Judg. 6:12b, 14b). Gideon did not feel like a warrior. He protested that his family was the poorest in the tribe of Manasseh and he himself the least in his father's house. But the Lord said, "Surely I will be with thee, and thou shalt smite the Midianites as one man" (Judg. 6:16b).

Following this exchange is the famous account where Gideon puts out his fleece to test whether the word he has received is truly from God (Judg. 6:36-40). Convinced at last that the Lord truly has spoken to him, Gideon goes out and rallies an army of 32,000 men. The Lord tells Gideon that he has too many men, and to let all who are afraid return home. Twenty-two thousand men leave (Judg. 7:1-3).

A test at the water's edge pares the army down to 300 men. Those who kneel to drink the water are sent home while those who remain watchful and use their hands to bring the water up to their mouths (300 do this) are retained as Gideon's army (Judg. 7:4-8). Gideon equips each of his men with a trumpet and a torch inside a clay pitcher and then divides them into three 100-man units. They are to deploy around the camp of the Midianites. Upon Gideon's signal, all 300 are to blow their trumpets, smash their pitchers so the torches can be seen, and shout, "The sword of the Lord and of Gideon!" (Judg. 7:16-18).

The unorthodox plan works to perfection. When the Midianites suddenly hear all these trumpets and shouts and see the light of many torches surrounding them, they flee in panic and in the ensuing confusion kill each other (Judg. 7:19-22).

Why did God tell Gideon to reduce his army from 32,000 to 300? For one thing, He wanted to make it clear to everyone that the victory was due to His power and not the size or military capability of Gideon's army. God was also weeding out all those who were not in agreement. Twenty-two thousand left out of fear, and fear is not in agreement with faith. The 9,700 who knelt to drink were released also, possibly because their posture while drinking betrayed a lack of seriousness—and therefore a lack of full agreement—for the task ahead of them. Those that remained—Gideon's 300—were in full agreement and faith with the plan, and when they all came into agreement with God, He brought the victory.

Like the battle of Jehoshaphat with the Moabites and Ammonites, Gideon's battle with the Midianites makes no sense from the standpoint of human strategy. Because it was God's strategy, however, it could not fail. First John 5:4 says: "For whatsoever is born of God overcometh the world: and this is the victory that overcometh the world, even our faith." All that was required for victory was to agree with God. The size, skill, and might of the enemy did not matter. Once the people of God came into agreement with God, their victory was inevitable.

Chariots of Fire

Like Jehoshaphat and Gideon, the prophet Elisha knew the security and victory that come with walking in agreement with God. As the prophetic successor to Elijah, Elisha had seen it all. He had seen fire fall from heaven. He had seen his master Elijah ascend to heaven in a chariot of fire. He had seen people raised from the dead. He had seen a small jar of oil continue to produce long after it should have been empty. Elisha had seen enough to be absolutely confident that God was in charge. Because he understood how the Spirit of God flows, and because he had been operating in that flow for a long time, Elisha lost his ability to get alarmed at external circumstances.

In Second Kings 6, the Syrians are trying to capture Elisha and bring him back to their king, because Elisha has been telling the king of Israel all of Syria's plans for attack. Learning that Elisha is in the city of Dothan, the Syrians completely surround the city with their chariots and horses. Early in the morning, Elisha's servant sees the surrounding army and is filled with fear. Rushing to Elisha, the servant cries out, "What are we going to do?"

Elisha possessed a degree of spiritual vision that his servant did not yet have. His reply reflects his unshakable confidence in the power and protection of God:

> *¹⁶And he answered, Fear not: for they that be with us are more than they that be with them. ¹⁷And Elisha prayed, and said, Lord, I pray thee, open his eyes, that he may see. And the Lord opened the eyes of the young man; and he saw: and, behold, the mountain was full of horses and chariots of fire round about Elisha* (2 Kings 6:16-17).

Finally, Elisha's servant understood that there was no reason to be afraid. As long as they walked with God, they were under His protection. No enemy could touch them, much less defeat them.

The Drawing Power of the Spirit

That which was true for Jehoshaphat, Gideon, Elisha, and many other people of faith in the Bible is also true for us. When we walk in faith, all our battles are won in the spirit before they ever reach the earth. The moment we set ourselves in agreement with God regarding any problem, obstacle, or battle, our victory is already won. It doesn't matter how grim or hopeless things may look. It doesn't matter what other people say. It doesn't matter whether or not we get three prophecies in line with it; the moment we line our heart and mind and will with God, we activate His promise and He wins the battle for us.

If we are to have any hope of changing the spiritual climate where we are, it is crucial that we understand the power that comes with being in agreement with God. When a spiritual climate is stamped in authority and in agreement, it carries the power to draw people to that purpose, sometimes for generations. This is true whether the climate is positive or negative. We have to get it into our spirit that we can come so into agreement with God that we can stamp our region with the power of the Holy Spirit to such a degree that people begin to choose to participate with the Spirit of God almost in spite of themselves.

The only thing the devil responds to is greater force or authority. When the Holy Spirit gets stamped on a region through the body of Christ coming into corporate agreement with God, that greater authority begins to push the devil out until a new climate comes in that is conducive for the Spirit of God. In that new environment, the Spirit can draw people who at first don't even know why they are being drawn or by whom.

A man may be sitting at home holding a gun to his head, ready to end it all. Suddenly some inner voice or prompting stops him. Instead of taking his own life, he finds himself strangely driven to seek out a pastor or a Christian friend or family member who will show him how to get right with God and give his life to Jesus. A woman with two small children who was abandoned by her husband and just lost her job suddenly finds herself drawn to pray for the first time in years. This man and woman, and thousands of others like them, are drawn by the Spirit to discover the life they were born for—a life lived as children of the living God—a life that for so long had been hidden from them and denied to them by the negative influence of an ungodly spiritual climate. Under the new climate of the Spirit of God, they are set free.

Isaiah chapter 43 contains an awesome promise from God regarding the power of God's people being in agreement with Him. We can literally change the climate wherever we are and see people in bondage set free and brought in to God's Kingdom to join us as fellow members of His family. Consider the words of the Lord:

> *¹But now thus saith the Lord that created thee, O Jacob, and he that formed thee, O Israel, Fear not: for I have redeemed thee, I have called thee by thy name; thou art mine. ²When thou passest through the waters, I will be with thee; and through the rivers, they shall not overflow thee: when thou walkest through the fire, thou shalt not be burned; neither shall the flame kindle upon thee. ³For I am the Lord thy God, the Holy One of Israel, thy Saviour: I gave Egypt for thy ransom, Ethiopia and Seba for thee. ⁴Since thou wast precious in my sight, thou hast been honourable, and I have loved thee: therefore will I give men for thee, and people for thy life. ⁵Fear not: for I am with thee: I will bring thy seed from the east, and gather thee from the west; ⁶I will say to the north, Give up; and to the south, Keep not back: bring my sons from far, and my daughters from the ends of the*

earth; [7]Even every one that is called by my name: for I have created him for my glory, I have formed him; yea, I have made him (Isaiah 43:1-7).

We are children of God and members of the body of Christ. This is our purpose in being; it is what we were created for. We belong to the Lord, and when we walk in agreement with Him, He will carry us through flood and through fire, give us the nations of the world as a "ransom," and through us draw the rest of the children home. As we come into agreement with God, we will change the climate where we are, and the Spirit will speak to the principalities and powers in the north, south, east, and west, saying, "Give up…Keep not back: bring my sons from afar, and my daughters from the ends of the earth."

This is our calling and our destiny. Let the Church get into corporate agreement with God and together we will change the spiritual climate wherever we are.

SECTION TWO

Image Changers

Captivity has made us think we are
outnumbered, outclassed, out-organized,
and out-gifted leaving us
feeling inferior and less than.

Chapter Four

The Babylonian Captivity
of the Church

According to most reports, the Sunday following the terrorist attacks of September 11, 2001 recorded perhaps the highest church attendance nationwide in the history of our country. In the wake of such a horrific tragedy many Americans instinctively felt they needed to be in church. Why? Because we are a nation of believers.

A similar but smaller rise in church attendance followed the loss of the space shuttle *Columbia* and its seven astronauts on February 1, 2003 as it disintegrated during reentry. Churches across America were filled and memorial services in Washington, Houston, Florida, and many other places were likewise well-attended. When disaster strikes, Americans turn to God because we are a nation of believers.

The longest sustained season of high church attendance in America was during the years of the Great Depression. Millions of Americans were out of work with little money or possessions and even less prospects of improving their circumstances. In a time of such great need and hardship, people went to church in large numbers seeking consolation from God. We are a nation of believers.

Even today in the opening years of the third millennium after Christ, America remains by far the most religious of all the industrialized nations of the world. Nationwide polls consistently show that 90% or more of Americans believe in God. A smaller yet still substantial majority regard themselves as "religious" or "spiritual" people whose religious beliefs play at least some part in their lives. We are a nation of believers.

Yet something is wrong with this picture. The spikes in church attendance that followed the September 11 attacks and the *Columbia* disaster proved to be short-lived. Within a few days or, at most, a few weeks, church attendance had dropped back to their pre-disaster levels. The interest in God and the Church shown by Depression-era Americans did not translate into a lasting spiritual awakening in our country. And despite the high percentage of Americans today who claim to believe in God, many have little or no ongoing involvement with the Church and their belief in God makes little practical difference in the way they live. We may be a nation of believers, but we are *not* a nation of *belongers*.

Most Americans believe in God, but a far smaller number claim membership or regular active involvement with any church. Some of them, in fact, wouldn't be caught dead inside the house of God. Others, however, attend faithfully every Christmas and Easter. Because they believe, many people attend churches they don't belong to, want to be married in churches they don't belong to, and want to be buried in churches they haven't darkened the doors of since they were born. They want their babies dedicated and baptized in church, but they don't belong. We are a nation of believers but not belongers.

How do we explain this inconsistency? What is it about American society and culture that make so many Americans reluctant to belong even though they claim to believe? Part of the answer has to do with who controls the public image of the Church.

Culture Clash

Life in our society today is characterized by a clash of cultures. On one side stands the culture of the Church and the people of God, while on the other stands the culture of the world, whose beliefs and values by and large run contrary to the nature and will of God. This culture clash takes shape in a battle over atmospheres and climates; a struggle for the very hearts and minds of Americans, including Christians.

One of the greatest challenges we face as Christians today is to avoid being seduced into adopting the beliefs, values, and ways of worldly culture. At the same time, we cannot simply separate ourselves from all contact with it. Throughout the history of the Church, believers in every generation have struggled with the problem of how to live *in* the world and yet not be *of* the world. How can the Church engage the world in a meaningful and relevant way while at the same time remaining true to Christ and keeping itself uncorrupted by the world's secular culture?

This culture clash, while contemporary, is not new. It has been going on for as long as God has had a people. The ancient Israelites struggled with it constantly. Even though they were God's chosen people, the people of the covenant through Abraham, Isaac, and Jacob, after 400 years of slavery in Egypt, they had a hard time leaving Egyptian culture and beliefs behind when Moses led them to freedom. Over and over they complained about the hardships of their new circumstances and expressed longing for the "flesh pots" of Egypt. Finally, when their rebellion reached a climax by their acceptance of a negative report by ten of the twelve spies Moses had dispatched to reconnoiter the land of Canaan and their subsequent refusal to enter the land, God had had enough. He condemned them to wander in the wilderness for 40 years until that entire rebellious generation had died. Of that generation, only Joshua and Caleb, the two spies who had remained true to God, lived to enter the Promised Land.

Even after Joshua led them into the land of Canaan, the Israelites still had problems dealing with the local culture. The subsequent history of Israel is a sad cycle of idolatry, judgment, repentance, and restoration repeated multiple times until finally their continued rebellion led to disaster. After Solomon's death, the nation of Israel divided into two parts: the Northern Kingdom of Israel, consisting of ten tribes, and the Southern Kingdom of Judah, which also included the tribe of Benjamin. In 722 B.C., the Northern Kingdom of Israel was conquered by the Assyrian Empire and disappeared from history. Almost a century-and-a-half later, in 587 B.C., the Southern Kingdom of Judah was defeated and taken into captivity by the Babylonian Empire, which had succeeded the Assyrians.

The Old Testament Book of Daniel dates from the period of the Babylonian exile and provides an excellent illustration of culture clash and the challenges it poses for the people of God in any generation.

Daniel was one of many young Jewish men taken to Babylon at the beginning of the captivity and groomed for service to the Babylonian king. From the outset he faced the challenge of dealing with the clash of cultures:

[1] In the third year of the reign of Jehoiakim king of Judah came Nebuchadnezzar king of Babylon unto Jerusalem,

and besieged it.... ³*And the king spake unto Ashpenaz the master of his eunuchs, that he should bring certain of the children of Israel, and of the king's seed, and of the princes;* ⁴*Children in whom was no blemish, but well favoured, and skilful in all wisdom, and cunning in knowledge, and understanding science, and such as had ability in them to stand in the king's palace, and whom they might teach the learning and the tongue of the Chaldeans.* ⁵*And the king appointed them a daily provision of the king's meat, and of the wine which he drank: so nourishing them three years, that at the end thereof they might stand before the king.* ⁶*Now among these were of the children of Judah, Daniel, Hananiah, Mishael, and Azariah:* ⁷*Unto whom the prince of the eunuchs gave names: for he gave unto Daniel the name of Belteshazzar; and to Hananiah, of Shadrach; and to Mishael, of Meshach; and to Azariah, of Abednego.*

⁸*But Daniel purposed in his heart that he would not defile himself with the portion of the king's meat, nor with the wine which he drank: therefore he requested of the prince of the eunuchs that he might not defile himself.* ⁹*Now God had brought Daniel into favour and tender love with the prince of the eunuchs.* ¹⁰*And the prince of the eunuchs said unto Daniel, I fear my lord the king, who hath appointed your meat and your drink: for why should he see your faces worse liking than the children which are of your sort? then shall ye make me endanger my head to the king.* ¹¹*Then said Daniel to Melzar, whom the prince of the eunuchs had set over Daniel, Hananiah, Mishael, and Azariah,* ¹²*Prove thy servants, I beseech thee, ten days; and let them give us pulse to eat, and water to drink.* ¹³*Then let our countenances be looked upon before thee, and the countenance of the*

children that eat of the portion of the king's meat: and as thou seest, deal with thy servants. ¹⁴So he consented to them in this matter, and proved them ten days. ¹⁵And at the end of ten days their countenances appeared fairer and fatter in flesh than all the children which did eat the portion of the king's meat. ¹⁶Thus Melzar took away the portion of their meat, and the wine that they should drink; and gave them pulse (Daniel 1:1, 3-16).

Here we see the classic conflict between the Kingdom of God and the powers of darkness. Often in the Bible kings represent spiritual powers. On the one hand is Jehoiakim, king of Judah and descendent of David; he represents the Kingdom and the people of God. The name "Judah" means "praise," so the people of Judah are the children of praise. They stand for God's culture, the culture of righteousness.

Facing off against the king of Judah is Nebuchadnezzar, king of Babylon, who represents the culture of the world, which is under the sway of Satan, the prince of the powers of darkness. Nebuchadnezzar's desire was to remove from Judah "certain of the children of Israel, and of the king's seed, and of the princes"—members of the royal family, in other words—and prepare them for service in his own court. They were to be the crème de la crème of Judah; the finest young men the kingdom had to offer, without blemish, handsome, skilled, wise, well-educated, and possessing the necessary poise and bearing to serve as direct aides and advisers to the king of Babylon. As part of their preparation, they were to be taught the "learning and the tongue of the Chaldeans." The king of Babylon even apportioned to them a daily allotment of his own meat and wine.

In the Bible, "meat" often symbolizes doctrine and "wine," spirit. Nebuchadnezzar sought to take the cream of Jewish manhood and fill them with his own doctrine—the value system of the world—and place upon them his own spirit, the spirit of the world.

From a more literal standpoint, the king's meat and wine contained elements that were not kosher for devout Jews such as Daniel and his three friends to partake of. This clash of cultures threatened to crush them in the middle. They faced a hard choice: either they could quietly submit and in so doing sacrifice their character and integrity, or they could resist and quite possibly lose their lives. Daniel and his friends were determined to find a way, to survive and thrive in the midst of a pagan culture while at the same time maintaining their character, integrity, and spiritual identity as obedient servants of God.

Notice how they handled the problem. They didn't rail out angrily in defiance, nor did they meekly give in. Instead, they took a diplomatic approach. Daniel, apparently speaking for all four of them, politely requested that they be exempted from consuming the king's food and drink so they would not defile themselves. When Ashpenaz, the chief of the king's eunuchs, expressed fear of losing his head if the king found out that he had failed in his responsibility, Daniel proposed a simple test. "Give us just vegetables and water for ten days," Daniel suggested to Melzar, Ashpenaz's subordinate, "and then see how we compare to the other young men who partake of the king's food and drink." Behind Daniel's request lay a confident belief that God would honor them for their faithfulness.

Melzar agreed to the proposal and the test began. For ten days Daniel and his three friends consumed nothing but vegetables and water. Daniel 1:15 records the result: "And at the end of ten days their countenances appeared fairer and fatter in flesh than all the children which did eat the portion of the king's meat." Seeing this, Melzar gave Daniel and his friends their vegetables and water diet on a continual basis.

Three years later, when their period of training and preparation was complete, Daniel and his friends were brought in to King Nebuchadnezzar. "And the king communed with them; and among them all was found none like Daniel, Hananiah, Mishael, and Azariah: therefore stood they before the king. And in all matters of wisdom and understanding, that the king inquired of them, he found them ten times better than all the magicians and astrologers that were in all his realm" (Dan. 1:19-20).

The king found Daniel and his friends to be *ten times better* in wisdom and understanding than all the pagan magicians and astrologers in his kingdom. It is significant to note that the smartest, wisest, best, most gifted, most talented, most skilled, and most competent people in this secular culture came not from that culture but from the people of God. God has always desired it to be this way. He has always wanted His people to set the standard for the rest of the world in character, integrity, knowledge, understanding, and excellence.

Unfortunately, in our modern society today, this is not the image that most people in the secular culture have of the Church. The reason for this is because the spirit of the secular culture controls the image of the Church in that culture.

Image Control

We live in a very image-conscious society. Current generations of people brought up on movies and television are more image- and visual-oriented than are earlier generations. Add desktops, laptops, and "palm pilots," and it becomes clear that we are surrounded by visual imagery of every kind.

Image also has to do with the way something is perceived. Our perception is shaped by how we think, and our way of thinking depends on the information and stimuli we receive from outside sources. Thinking involves imagination, and the root word of imagination is the word "image." In other words, our perception of something depends on how we "image" it in our minds. Our "imaging" (or "imagining") depends on our thinking, which depends on the information we receive. Therefore, whoever controls the information we receive about a thing controls the image we have of that thing.

Kings, emperors, dictators, and other rulers have understood this for centuries. Control people's access to information and you control what they think. If you control what people think, it is much easier to get them to do what you want them to do. That is the principle behind propaganda, or behind "slanting" the news: controlling access to information in order to cause people to think—and then act—a certain way.

This is just how Satan operates in our world. He works in our minds, seeking to shape our thoughts and our imaginings so that we will see things the way he wants us to see them, rather than seeing them the way God sees them. Satan seeks image control because he knows that if he can control our perceptions, he can control our responses.

In Second Corinthians 10:5 Paul says that we are to "[cast] down imaginations, and every high thing that exalteth itself against the knowledge of God, and [bring] into captivity every thought to the obedience of Christ." In other words, if we resist Satan and break his control over information concerning a thing, we can change the image of that thing not only in our own minds but also in the minds of others.

Once again, the Book of Daniel provides an excellent illustration. Just because Daniel and his three friends Shadrach, Meshach, and Abednego passed their first test with regard to not defiling themselves with the king's food and drink did not mean their problems were over. Before long, thanks to Nebuchadnezzar's arrogance, they faced an even greater challenge.

¹Nebuchadnezzar the king made an image of gold, whose height was threescore cubits, and the breadth thereof six cubits: he set it up in the plain of Dura, in the province of Babylon.... ⁴Then an herald cried aloud, To you it is commanded, O people, nations, and languages, ⁵That at what time ye hear the sound of the cornet, flute, harp, sackbut, psaltery, dulcimer, and all kinds of music, ye fall down and worship the golden image that Nebuchadnezzar the king hath set up: ⁶And whoso falleth not down and worshippeth shall the same hour be cast into the midst of a burning fiery furnace. ⁷Therefore at that time, when all the people heard the sound of the cornet, flute, harp, sackbut, psaltery, and all kinds of music, all the people, the nations, and the languages, fell down and worshipped the golden image that Nebuchadnezzar the king had set up (Daniel 3:1, 4-7).

The gloves had come off; the gauntlet had been thrown down. Nebuchadnezzar thought he was "the man." After all, he ruled over the most powerful empire the world had ever seen. Could he not do whatever he pleased? Didn't everybody have to obey his every whim? The Babylonian king was into image control big-time. An image of gold was made according to his specifications (90 feet tall and 9 feet wide), set up in the plain of Dura according to his direction, and established as the supreme god of Babylon before which all subjects in his kingdom were to bow in worship. Any who refused would be burned to death in the king's own furnace. Who would dare defy the all-powerful Nebuchadnezzar in this matter?

Three of the Hebrew exiles did. Word reached Nebuchadnezzar that three of his most trusted advisers, Hananiah (Shadrach), Mishael (Meshach), and Azariah (Abednego) had refused to worship the king's golden image. They refused to buy into the secular culture that would force them to betray their God.

Infuriated at this news of defiance, the arrogant king ordered the three men brought before him. He offered them a second chance:

> *14Nebuchadnezzar spake and said unto them, Is it true, O Shadrach, Meshach, and Abednego, do not ye serve my gods, nor worship the golden image which I have set up? 15Now if ye be ready that at what time ye hear the sound of the cornet, flute, harp, sackbut, psaltery, and dulcimer, and all kinds of music, ye fall down and worship the image which I have made; well: but if ye worship not, ye shall be cast the same hour into the midst of a burning fiery furnace; and who is that God that shall deliver you out of my hands?"* (Daniel 3:14-15)

Can you believe the arrogance of Nebuchadnezzar's last question? He was so caught up in his own power and self-importance that he believed that there was no god anywhere that could stand up to him. (This is also what he wanted all the people in his kingdom to believe. That's what image control is all about.)

Shadrach, Meshach, and Abednego knew better. With supreme faith and confidence in the absolute sovereignty and omnipotence of their God, the God of Israel, the three Hebrew men stood up to the king of Babylon:

> *16Shadrach, Meshach, and Abednego, answered and said to the king, O Nebuchadnezzar, we are not careful to answer thee in this matter. 17If it be so, our God whom we serve is able to deliver us from the burning fiery furnace, and he will deliver us out of thine hand,*

O king. ¹⁸But if not, be it known unto thee, O king,
that we will not serve thy gods, nor worship the golden
image which thou hast set up (Daniel 3:16-18).

The Bible says that after this response Nebuchadnezzar
was "full of fury" and "his visage was changed" toward the three
men. In other words, he did not look favorably upon them as
he once had. Instead, he ordered the furnace heated seven times
hotter than usual and that Shadrach, Meshach, and Abednego
be thrown into it. Nebuchadnezzar thought he was in control,
but he was about to learn that things are not always as they appear:

²⁴Then Nebuchadnezzar the king was astonied, and
rose up in haste, and spake, and said unto his counsel-
lors, Did not we cast three men bound into the midst of
the fire? They answered and said unto the king, True,
O king. ²⁵He answered and said, Lo, I see four men
loose, walking in the midst of the fire, and they have no
hurt; and the form of the fourth is like the Son of God
(Daniel 3:24-25).

Astonished that they had survived the fires of the furnace—
and had obviously received divine protection—Nebuchadnezzar called to the three Hebrew men, referring to them with
new respect as "servants of the most high God," and ordered
them out of the furnace. Not only had Shadrach, Meshach, and
Abednego come through the fire completely unscathed, they
did not even have the smell of smoke or fire on them. Witnessing this miracle of deliverance changed Nebuchadnezzar's
whole perspective. He now understood that there *was* a God
who could deliver people out of his hand. The king responded
with awe and reverence—and a new edict:

> *28 Then Nebuchadnezzar spake, and said, Blessed be the God of Shadrach, Meshach, and Abednego, who hath sent his angel, and delivered his servants that trusted in him, and have changed the king's word, and yielded their bodies, that they might not serve nor worship any god, except their own God. 29 Therefore I make a decree, That every people, nation, and language, which speak any thing amiss against the God of Shadrach, Meshach, and Abednego, shall be cut in pieces, and their houses shall be made a dunghill: because there is no other God that can deliver after this sort. 30 Then the king promoted Shadrach, Meshach, and Abednego, in the province of Babylon (Daniel 3:28-30).*

In light of what he had witnessed, the king of Babylon changed his tune. Instead of boasting that there was no god who could deliver from his hand, Nebuchadnezzar now blessed the God of Israel and forbade, on pain of death, anyone in the kingdom from speaking ill of Him.

By all appearances, Nebuchadnezzar controlled the image-making mechanism in Babylon. Shadrach, Meshach, and Abednego knew this was not so. Because they knew who they were—children and servants of the most high God—and because they understood the power of the God they served, they defied the king, stood up against the prevailing culture, and *changed the image.*

Shadrach, Meshach, and Abednego were Hebrews living in covenant with the God of their fathers, the God of Abraham, Isaac, and Jacob. Nebuchadnezzar, the image-maker of the secular culture, sought to turn them into Babylonians. He failed because they refused to accept the image he tried to impose on them. Instead, they looked beyond that image and fixed their eyes and their hopes on the God of truth who could cast down all false images.

The same thing happened to Daniel in chapter six when he defied a foolish edict of King Darius and ended up in the lions' den. Darius had issued a decree that for 30 days no one in the kingdom could pray to anyone except him. Like his predecessor Nebuchadnezzar, Darius was trying to control the image. Daniel's defiance earned him a night with the lions. Once again, however, the Lord delivered His faithful servant and once again a pagan king learned who the *real* image-maker was. After Daniel emerged unharmed from the lions' den, Darius issued another decree "That in every dominion of my kingdom men tremble and fear before the God of Daniel: for he is the living God, and steadfast for ever, and his kingdom that which shall not be destroyed, and his dominion shall be even unto the end" (Dan. 6:26).

The Church of "Less-Than"

The challenge facing the Church today with regard to the dominant culture is very similar to the one that Daniel, Shadrach, Meshach, and Abednego faced with the Babylonian Empire of their day. Like them, we face the danger of being "Babylonianized." Unlike them, we have in many ways been unsuccessful in resisting or changing the image of the Church that our secular culture has erected.

Image-making in our culture is controlled, for the most part, by forces that are hostile—or at least unsympathetic—to the Church. The prevailing spirit of our age stands in opposition to God, which is why so many parts of our nation, as well as many other nations, are under spiritual climates and strongholds that keep people in spiritual blindness. One way the enemy opposes the Church is by creating an image of the

Church as weak, powerless, and irrelevant, with no critical or meaningful role to play in modern society. More and more he seeks to paint the Church as a place for losers, a place filled with dysfunctional and broken-down people who have no where else to go.

Don't get me wrong; the Church *is* a place for those who have suffered loss. All of us have lost before we found Christ; that's what it means to say we are "lost." The Church *is* a place for us to bring our faults and our failures and our flaws and our weaknesses and our dysfunctions—not so we can wallow in them or be coddled in them, but so we can be healed and delivered of them! Jesus said we should *come* as we are, not that we should *stay* as we are. The ministry of the Church is to mend the broken, heal the sick, lift up the fallen, strengthen the weak, and encourage the downhearted. Our mission is not simply to bring people to Jesus and leave them there. Jesus commissioned us not to make believers but to make *disciples*: disciplined learners and followers who grow to maturity in faith and character and become leaders, prophetic voices, and influential examples in their communities. The Church is where all the best "movers and shakers" in the world should be found. The Church should set the standard for the world in excellence and leadership in every area.

Unfortunately, such a living, dynamic organism is not the image most of the world has of the Church. Just as Nebuchadnezzar did with the Jewish exiles, the enemy seeks to pull out of the Church (or prevent from entering) all those who are gifted, wise, skillful, motivated, goal-oriented, artistic, musical, entrepreneurial, business-minded, well-educated, intellectually sharp, and articulate and "Babylonianize" them. He wants to take the cream of the crop of the Church and win them over to the beliefs and values of the popular culture. If he can convince them (and everybody else) that the Church is no place for people with their gifts and talents, he can create the impression in their minds that the Church is made up of nothing but a bunch of "duds." Rather than a dynamic, living organism possessing the power to transform the world, the body of Christ becomes in the eyes of the world the Church of "less than."

What's even worse is that this same attitude of "less than" has infiltrated the Church. Many Christians have bought into the imagery of Nebuchadnezzar, which has produced in much of the body of Christ a spirit of insecurity and inferiority. Unfortunately, much of the religious teaching in the Church today reinforces this mentality. We are told that as Christians we are aliens in enemy territory; transients on earth rather than possessors of the land. We are told that we should just be quiet, circle the wagons while the world increases against us and valiantly "hold the fort" until Jesus returns to rescue us from our peril.

We are made to think we are outnumbered, outclassed, out-organized, and out-gifted, leaving us feeling inferior and less than. One big reason people believe but don't belong is because we as the body of Christ do not know how to break the image that the power of the air has used against us.

Essentially, image control is mind control because our minds operate on imagery. Proverbs 23:7 says that as a man "thinketh in his heart, so is he." In other words, our sense of identity and self-worth depends on how we think about ourselves, and how we think about ourselves depends on the image we have accepted. Generally, the image we have of ourselves is the image we project to other people.

If you imagine yourself as a loser you will be a loser. You will never become a winner until you change your image of yourself in your own mind and begin to see yourself as a winner. On the other hand, if you see yourself as a winner, you are a winner, regardless of what your current circumstances may say. Once you have set your mind on victory, no one can defeat you, not even the devil. The great thing about imagination is that even in the midst of defeat or in the middle of the worst circumstances of life we can imagine ourselves as overcomers on the other side of it all, and that image can sustain us until we actually get there.

The Babylonian Captivity of the Church

Much of the body of Christ today is caught up in what I call the "Babylonian captivity of the Church." In this sense, captivity is different than bondage. Let's use the nation of Israel as an illustration. Prior to the time of Moses, the children of Israel spent 400 years in bondage as slaves to the Egyptians. Egyptian bondage was just that—bondage. In Egypt there were chains. In Egypt there were taskmasters. In Egypt they had to labor hard from sunrise to sunset with little personal reward. In Egypt they were told when to rise, when to eat, and when to go to sleep. In Egypt, they could not do as they pleased or go where they pleased. In Egypt, every facet and every aspect of their life was strictly controlled by someone else. For the Israelites, Egypt was a place of narrow confinement and extreme limitation, a close place with walls on every side.

By analogy to the Church today, "Egyptian bondage" represents to us the life of addiction, the life of perversion, the life of out-of-control emotions, dysfunction, and anger—all the kinds of things that Jesus came to free us from. Part of the activity of the Church is the ministry of deliverance through which people are brought to Jesus, born again, and delivered from the things that hold them in bondage. By and large, the Church as a whole is pretty good at dealing with bondage.

Captivity is another story. When the exiles of the fallen Southern Kingdom of Judah were taken into Babylon, they began a 70-year period of captivity. Unlike Egypt, there were no chains or taskmasters. The exiles lived in their own homes and operated their own trades. Many, such as Daniel and his three friends, served in prominent positions in the Babylonian government. Except for the fact that they could not return physically to their homeland, the Jewish exiles basically controlled their own lives.

Their captivity was a captivity of the *mind*. Seventy years under a pervasive pagan culture was bound to have an influence. Many of the Jewish refugees became so "Babylonianized" during their exile that when they had an opportunity under Cyrus the Persian to return home, they didn't want to go. Life in Babylon had grown too comfortable and familiar. Essentially, they had made their peace with the culture and had adopted many of its beliefs, values, and customs. Physically, they were free to go, but their minds held them captive in the land of their exile.

Today, "Babylonian captivity" represents imprisonment of the mind. If I can convince you to believe a certain thing and think a certain way, I can control your actions without somebody standing over you. That's the way the enemy works in the culture. He seeks to control or manipulate our actions by controlling how we think. He attempts to control our thoughts and mental processes by seducing and enticing and tempting us with the beliefs, values, customs, and practices of the greater culture. If we buy into the philosophy and worldview of the secular culture, we become "Babylonianized" and lose our identity as a distinct counterculture.

This is the Church generation that we live in today. We are children of the Promise, called to a life of dominion, sacrifice, and worship. Yet for many of us life in the larger culture is so good that we are satisfied where we are. As long as we can be "Babylonian," we'd rather take a pass on the higher demands and disciplines of the Christian life. It's fine to be a Christian as long as it does not interfere with the comfort, pleasure, and success of our "Babylonian" lifestyle. If faced with a choice between following Jesus as a committed disciple and staying in Babylon, we'd just as soon stay in Babylon.

After all, life is easier in Babylon. There is less personal sacrifice required and fewer inconvenient time demands. Moral and ethical standards are lower and nobody expects complete honesty in every situation. Religion—even Christianity—is comfortable and acceptable in Babylon—as long as no one takes it *too* seriously or becomes *too* radical or *too* fanatical about it.

While the Church may be good at getting people out of "Egyptian" bondage, we're not as effective in freeing them from their "Babylonian" captivity. Sometimes it's because we're caught up in it ourselves. How can a captive free another captive? We simply don't know how to deliver a generation that has been enslaved in their minds, particularly when we too are part of that generation.

No matter how comfortable we may be in Babylon, no matter how much the principalities and powers of the air entice us to adopt the ways of this world, and no matter how easy it is simply to conform to the standards of the dominant culture around us, that is not our calling. God did not call us to a life of ease that is devoid of sacrifice, commitment, and discipline. He did not call us to a life where we remain spoiled spiritual infants craving nothing more than the simplest spiritual "milk" while despising the "meat,"—the full spiritual nourishment of the deeper things of God and His Word. God did not call us to a life devoid of prayer and fasting. He did not call us to live our lives the way we see fit, becoming gods unto ourselves and serving the gods of this generation while ignoring His house and His Kingdom.

No! God called us to a life of disciplined, mature, faithful, confident, and joyful obedience through which He can establish His power and His Kingdom in the earth.

The Church has an image problem. Much of the world sees the Church as weak, irrelevant, inferior, outdated, and completely out of touch with modern society. They regard us as the Church of "less-than," a bunch of losers who possess nothing that the world either needs or desires. Until the body of Christ as a whole stops agreeing with that assessment; until we are determined to break out of the "Babylonian captivity" of our minds, we will never change our image, much less change the world. All over the world, "power shifting" churches and "breakthrough" people have to deal with the image of inferiority and irrelevance that the principalities and powers of the air have set up in an effort to keep people from belonging. We must become "breakthrough" people.

If we want "breakthrough," if we want to shatter the world's false image of the Church and replace it with the truth, we have to become like Shadrach, Meshach and Abednego and be willing to walk through some heat. We have to become like Daniel and be prepared to face the lions of adversity. We have to stop being ashamed to speak up about what God is doing in our lives! We have to be willing to say, "I'm not going to eat of the doctrine or drink of the spirit of this present age because I have true nourishment from a better and higher source, a source this world knows nothing of, a source that will make me 'ten times better' than anybody who feeds on the world's food."

God always has people who can outdo what their counterparts in the world can do. These are people who are not lazy or defeated or broken down or inferior, but who maintain an excellent spirit. And when they break through, they change the image.

This is our calling. When we become image changers, the world will know that the Church is a people of power, not weakness; a people of relevance, not insignificance; a people of excellence, not mediocrity, and a people of life, not death. It's time for us to break out of the mental shackles of our "Babylonian captivity." It's time for us to become *image-changers.*

Many have resigned themselves to life

in a culture shaped by the secular and

humanistic voices in society rather than by

the prophetic voice of the church.

Chapter Five

Image Changers

Somewhere along the line the contemporary church in America has developed a defeatist mentality. We have bought into society's erroneous image of the Church as impotent, irrelevant, and outmoded. No one, we are told, with any real brains, gifts, or talents will waste those assets in church life when they can achieve greater success and acclaim serving the popular culture. Many Christians have lived for so long in the shadow of defeat with no clear sign in their midst of God's presence and power that they have accepted such a state of affairs as the norm. Many have resigned themselves to life in a culture shaped by the secular and humanistic voices in society rather than by the prophetic voice of the Church. Society is prepared to tolerate the Church as long as it keeps its mouth shut about "issues" and focuses its attention on dealing with the broken-down, beat-up, busted and disgusted, dysfunctional people.

As James 3:10 says, "My brethren, these things ought not so to be." There is no place in the Church of Christ or in the people of God for a defeatist mindset. The Bible says we are winners, not losers. Rather than a defeated people, we are "more than conquerors" through Christ who loves us (Rom. 8:37). When Jesus established His Church He promised that the gates of hell would not prevail against it (Matt. 16:18). There is no defeat in Jesus Christ. No matter what our situation or circumstance, in Christ we already have the victory. Ultimately, everything will serve His purpose and our good if we love Him and are committed to obeying Him. That is why Paul says, "All things work together for good to them that love God, to them who are the called according to his purpose" (Rom. 8:28). In other words, someday God will cause even our mistakes to glorify Him. It's a given: as Christians, we cannot lose!

So why then do we act like losers? Why do we continue in a defeatist mindset that reinforces the cultural image of the Church as nothing more than a refuge for the dregs of society, a place of "less-than"? Is it because we have come to believe that image? Is it because we don't expect anything more from our Christian life or from the ministry of the Church? Is it because we have somehow accepted the idea that this is how the Church is supposed to be?

We will never change society's image of the Church until we lay aside our defeatist mentality and start thinking and acting like winners. To begin with, we must stop being merely believers and become true belongers; we must buy into the work that God is doing all around us to cast down strongholds and change images. Until and unless we as children of God take personal ownership of God's purposes in the earth, we will never pose a threat to the powers of darkness in our generation. Contrary to what the world thinks, Christians are not helpless, powerless, poverty-stricken orphans. We are children and heirs of the eternal King of kings with all His resources at our disposal. It's time for us to become who we were meant to be!

As children of the King, we are called to be disciples: disciplined ones, ethical ones, principled ones, learning ones. Believers are not necessarily belongers, but only belongers can become disciples. Our Lord has charged us with a sacred trust—His Kingdom on earth—but He cannot entrust His Kingdom to those who are ignorant of its nature and its principles and who have never taken personal ownership of it.

The Church is a community of faith; a body of people bound together in a "common unity" of faith in Christ, to whom He has entrusted stewardship of the earth. He has entrusted and charged us not merely to speak *about* Him but to speak *for* Him in the midst of our communities. Christ established His Church to ensure that He has a continuing witness in the earth, and that witness He has entrusted to His disciples—those who have committed themselves to be belongers and not just believers. As stewards of this sacred trust, we are answerable to God for our stewardship.

Jesus told us to go and "teach (make disciples of) all nations" (Matt. 28:19). It takes *belonging*. As belongers, disciples have taken ownership of what they believe. Not only are they *professors* of the truth; they are also *possessors* of the truth. They know what they believe and why they believe it. They can, therefore, proceed with secure confidence when they talk to someone about their faith. This is in keeping with Peter's instruction to "be ready always to give an answer to every man that asketh you a reason for the hope that is in you..." (1 Pet. 3:15). Anyone who feels uncertain or insecure about their faith will lack the power to persuade others.

Called to Proclaim the Sovereignty of God

Part of the mission of the Church is to declare that God reigns in heaven *and* on earth. "Babylonian" mentality seeks to relegate God's authority to heaven only and convince people that He has no authority or jurisdiction in this world. This is part of the false image. If God is irrelevant to the affairs of mankind on the earth, then so are His children, the Church that represents His Name.

The Bible, however, plainly states that God is Lord of all: heaven and earth, the spiritual and the physical, the supernatural and the natural. Paul says in Acts 17:24, "God that made the world and all things therein…is Lord of heaven and earth." Psalm 24:1 declares, "The earth is the Lord's, and all it contains, The world, and those who dwell in it." In Isaiah 66:1 God says, "The heaven is my throne, and the earth is my footstool."

As Christians our victory is assured, but that victory is founded firmly on the truth that God rules on earth as well as in heaven. This is a critical truth we must understand if we hope to be image changers. As long as God's authority on earth is still in question in our minds, we cannot exercise authority here either because we are insecure and unsure of the decisions that we make. If, on the other hand, we are confident that God reigns on earth as He does in heaven, we can move forward with boldness and authority to tear down strongholds and change images.

We are called to proclaim the sovereignty of God over both heaven and earth. This message directly opposes both Satan's claim to be lord of the earth as well as the popular notion that mankind apart from God is master of the world. The sovereignty of God over heaven and earth is a truth that the world resists—sometimes violently—because the deceived mind of man is bound by the mental strongholds of the powers of darkness and because the prideful heart of man refuses to recognize an authority higher than himself.

Many Christians have been taught that Satan is the owner of the earth. They never see any signs of God's sovereignty over the earth because they don't expect to see any. Their eyes are not trained to discern the activity of God. Satan has clouded their vision, leaving the impression that he is in unchallenged command. Meanwhile, the Kingdom of God is advancing throughout the earth. God's Kingdom is very real and active on the earth but is mainly unseen because it resides in the hearts of all who have been born again by the Spirit of God.

The Bible teaches that the Kingdom of God is held in a mystery and is presently invisible. No one can see it or enter it except by being born again. God's Kingdom does not consist of bricks and mortar. It has no physical walls or ceilings and boasts of no grand palaces of stone or treasuries of gold and silver and precious jewels. The Kingdom of God is an invisible Kingdom, at least for now. It is a treasure hidden in "earthen vessels"—the physical bodies of all who have placed their faith in Christ (2 Cor. 4:7). Today the Kingdom of God is manifest wherever the rulership of Christ is recognized and responded to. Wherever there are children of the King who exalt Him as Lord and in whose hearts He dwells as a living presence, His Kingdom is there.

At the return of Christ God's Kingdom will be visible and become evident to all people everywhere. On that day, "at the name of Jesus every knee [will] bow, of things in heaven, and things in earth, and things under the earth; and…every tongue [will] confess that Jesus Christ is Lord, to the glory of God the Father" (Phil. 2:10-11). When the King shows up, that which has been invisible will be made visible to all! What began with pressing and tribulation will end with the manifestation of glory. All that has been hidden will be revealed. God's Kingdom is already here, and we are moving toward its full revelation on the earth.

Until ultimate fulfillment, the mission of the Church is to proclaim the Kingdom of God as an everlasting Kingdom and the Lordship of Christ as a reign that will extend forever. This is the good news of the gospel: Jesus is Lord! Today He rules and reigns through His people who establish His authority wherever they put the sole of their feet by putting the enemy out and establishing the culture of the Kingdom.

Changing a Bad Impression

Few things in life are harder to overcome than a negative first impression. No matter how well we behave or how positively we present ourselves afterwards, that first meeting is what people will remember the most.

As Christians desiring to be image changers, we cannot afford to forget this fact. Generally speaking, the larger part of culture today has a false and negative impression of the Church and of Christians in general. Many of them regard Christians as naïve, ignorant, narrow-minded, intolerant, judgmental, and condemning losers who are stuck in the past and are therefore irrelevant and out of touch with the needs of modern society. We must change this impression before we can hope to be effective in proclaiming the Kingdom of God and making disciples.

In order for this to happen, we must learn, on both the personal and corporate levels, how to relate effectively to people. Too often in the Church we neglect the importance of basic people skills. No matter how gifted we are or how good we are at what we do, if we cannot relate to other people in a positive manner, whether in or out of the church, we're not going to get very far. The world is not impressed by a church filled with people who fight and bicker all the time. If we can't get along with each other, how can we hope to reach a lost world? Nonbelievers also do not respond favorably when we appear arrogant, obnoxious, hard-edged, or judgmental toward them. That's not the way to win them over. We have to learn how to relate to them—to touch them where they are.

Jesus was great at dealing with people. With fisherman, He talked about fishing. When He called four fishermen to be His disciples, He even told them they would become "fishers of men." With farmers, He spoke of sowing seed. Meeting a woman who had come to draw water from a well, Jesus spoke to her about living water. Everything Jesus did was relational because He was interested in people, and that's how we should be.

The Kingdom of God is established through covenant and relationship and is spread from person to person. It's not enough just to know the Bible inside and out. It's not enough just to be Spirit-filled or to be highly-gifted. Unless we know how to empathize and relate to people where they are, we will have little success in establishing the influence of God in their lives or in the culture as a whole.

So let's discuss a few basic people skills.

The first of these is *diligence*. Diligence is related to hard work and perseverance and is the opposite of laziness or slothfulness. Unfortunately, many church people are not very diligent. At least, that is the popular image among many nonbelievers.

Hebrews 11:6 says, "But without faith it is impossible to please [God]: for he that cometh to God must believe that he is, and that he is a rewarder of them that diligently seek him." Notice that last phrase: God rewards those who *diligently seek Him*. Diligence is a quality of mature Christian character. Diligent people do not make promises or commitments lightly, but when they do commit, they are faithful to follow through. They stick around until the job is done. They refuse to give less than their best and labor faithfully no matter what unexpected difficulties may come along.

The secular world values and respects personal diligence and hard work as keys to success, which it usually defines as wealth and material gain. Likewise, the Church must value and demonstrate diligence, but for a different reason: all our work should be done as an offering and an act of worship to God, and He is worthy of our very best.

A second important people skill is *decisiveness*. Few things are more frustrating than a person—and especially a leader—who can't make a decision. Sometimes indecision stems from a lack of confidence or uncertainty as to the extent of one's knowledge or authority. Indecision sometimes arises from fear of making the wrong decision. In such a situation it seems less risky simply not to decide. If we hope to touch people in the culture with the good news of the gospel, we must be confident in who we are, what we believe, and the power and authority we have in Christ. We can't afford to be afraid to make decisions when we have the position and responsibility to do so. If our hearts are right before God, He can take even our wrong decisions and turn them to His purpose and glory.

Decisiveness also means not changing our minds back and forth. Once we make a decision or adopt a certain position, we should stand firm. Jesus said, "But let your communication be, Yea, yea; Nay, nay: for whatsoever is more than these cometh of evil" (Matt. 5:37). James 5:12 echoes the same idea: "But above all things, my brethren, swear not, neither by heaven, neither by the earth, neither by any other oath: but let your yea be yea; and your nay, nay; lest ye fall into condemnation."

In other words, when we say yes, it ought to mean yes and when we say no, it ought to mean no. This does not mean we should be obstinate or stubborn at all costs. We should always be ready to change if we find that we are clearly wrong. It *does* mean that our word should be our bond with no wavering or flip-flopping. How can we reach or lead other people if they never know where we stand?

Along with diligence and decisiveness goes *discretion*. We shouldn't tell everybody everything we are doing. Some people don't need to know. Telling the wrong people—or even the right people at the wrong time or in the wrong way—can be disastrous. Look what happened to Joseph when he bragged to his jealous brothers about his dream in which they all bowed down to him. He ended up spending 20 years as a slave in Egypt. In the end, of course, it turned out well for Joseph as he became prime minister of Egypt, but the point is that as a youth he probably was not as discrete as he should have been, and it got him into trouble.

We should measure our speech and the information we give out, being careful to tell people just what they need to know. I'm not talking about being secretive or manipulative, but about being discrete. This means being sensitive to people's needs and where they are spiritually in their ability to understand. Don't answer questions they're not asking. Some people aren't ready for solid food yet; they're still drinking milk. Those who are just getting into the basics cannot yet handle the deeper things of God. Be discrete. Don't overload people or they will burn out.

When we do speak, we should exercise *diplomacy*. Diplomacy simply means saying the right thing the right way. Someone described diplomacy as the art of convincing others to do what you want and causing them to think that it was their idea. Truth is important, but what good is speaking the truth when no one listens because they are offended by the way we say it?

The Bible tells us to speak the truth in love (Eph. 4:15). We cannot use our love for others as an excuse not to tell them the truth. At the same time, we cannot use our obligation to speak the truth as an excuse not to treat others with love. Some Christians act as though they think that as long as they're speaking the truth—as long as they're right—it doesn't matter how they say it. That's not what God's Word says. We are to speak the truth in love and that means speaking diplomatically.

Even when we speak diplomatically, we must also learn to speak with *directness*. It's okay to be direct. People should never leave our presence wondering what we were talking about. If we're not clear in our communication, they have every right to say, "I don't understand." Directness does not necessarily mean bluntness (although bluntness may sometimes be in order). The key factor in directness is *clarity*—speaking in such a way that people understand what we say and what we mean. It is possible to speak directly and diplomatically at the same time and that should be our goal.

Understand the Purpose of Process

These five basic people skills are vital for our effectiveness in reaching others, but they are not enough by themselves to alter our culture. There are also several key principles that we must learn; principles that we must internalize and allow to become thoroughly settled in our spirit if we hope to become true image changers where we are.

First of all, we must understand the purpose of process. God is in the process of processing us. We tend to be outcome-conscious, while God is process-conscious. We just want to know the outcome. God wants to know what type of people we will become on our way to the outcome. This difference in perspective is due to what is in question. For us, the future is a mystery, so we sometimes question the outcome of our lives. God is not outcome-conscious because the outcome is not in question. Instead, He is process-conscious because He is most interested in seeing how we respond to life in process.

Outcome-consciousness is a sign that we do not understand the purpose of process. Questioning our outcome means that ultimately we doubt our "out-from." Once we understand our "out-from," it becomes clear that our outcome is already settled. If we know that we have "come out" from God, we can be confident that our outcome is assured in His hands. Romans 8:28 promises that "all things work together for good to them that love God, to them who are the called according to his purpose." Speaking of Christian believers in their conflict with Satan, Revelation 12:11 prophesies, "And they overcame him by the blood of the Lamb, and by the word of their testimony; and they loved not their lives unto the death." If we are "in Christ," to use Paul's phrase from Ephesians, our outcome is assured because He always causes us to triumph. The only thing in question is the particular path we take to get there.

What then is the purpose of process? All the things we go through in life, our struggles and hardships, our victories and defeats, our joys and sorrows, every experience whether good or bad, are all part of the process by which God prepares us to sit in the place of authority. The process then becomes just as important as the destination, because it is the journey itself that makes us ready for what God has called us to do.

Once we understand the power of the process, we realize that nothing happens to us by accident. Nothing enters our world that hasn't already passed through God's heart. Knowing this truth can transform the way we look at life. If we have committed our lives to Christ, He can and will use all our experiences, good and bad, to shape us into His likeness and mold us into the people He wants us to be. It is when we can look back over our life and identify the hand of God even in the uncomfortable situations that we realize that our life is one unbroken process of God working in us and maturing us so that He can launch us into our greatest destiny. That is the power of process.

Understand the Secret of Source

If we want to be image changers we must also understand the secret of source. We must know where our resources come from. Most people live their entire lives without a clue as to the true source of their supply. They depend on a company or another person for a paycheck and look to money to bring them security and happiness. The fact that God might be their source never crosses their minds.

Whenever we look to another person as our source of supply or self-esteem, we're on dangerous ground! As long as we depend on someone else to fulfill all of our needs, our needs will go unmet. What is the secret of source? It is that "every good gift and every perfect gift is from above, and cometh down from the Father of lights, with whom is no variableness, neither shadow of turning" (James 1:17). God is our source; the source of our strength, the source of our wisdom, the source of our joy, and the source of our peace. He is the source of all our supply.

Once we understand the secret of source we realize that it doesn't matter where we are because we always have a supply. Regardless of our situation, we can always tap into the river of living water, that wellspring of divine life and light that provides us with everything we need.

Understand the Power of Partnership

Another principle we need to understand if we want to be image changers is the power of partnership. All good things flow through relationship. Anything we can do by ourselves and that does not require the involvement of anyone else is a very small vision. If God calls you to do something and puts a vision in your heart, rest assured He will also plant complimentary talents in somebody else's life also. God is in the business of assigning God-sized tasks. In other words, when God gives us a vision, it will be a vision of something that only He can do. He wants to accomplish His will and purpose through us as we work together in community as the body of Christ and as we trust Him both individually and corporately.

None of us live our lives entirely by ourselves. All of us are involved in partnerships of one kind or another. Marriage is a partnership. Every local church is a partnership. A club is a partnership. Anyone we associate with on a regular basis for a common cause or purpose becomes a partner in that endeavor. Deciding who we partner with is very important because of the biblical principle of association, which says that we will become like the people we associate with. The Bible says, "He that walketh with wise men shall be wise: but a companion of fools shall be destroyed" (Prov. 13:20).

Do you want to become a loser? Hang out with losers. Do you want to become successful? Spend time with successful people. Pick their brains. Learn their secrets. Find out what makes them tick. Do you want to become more like Jesus? Take time to get to know Him. Devote yourself to His Word and to prayer. Because we are social creatures, we grow and thrive and succeed best when we are in partnership with others of like mind and vision. Simply stated, we need each other.

Daniel understood the power of partnership. When the king of Babylon threatened to kill all his wise men (including Daniel and his friends) unless someone told him both his dream and its interpretation, Daniel called on his three friends to pray. As Shadrach, Meshach, and Abednego interceded, Daniel went to the king and in the power of the Spirit answered the king's demand. The partnership in the Spirit of these four Hebrew men moved heaven and brought revelation to an earthly king.

A partner is someone who will go through the fire with you, someone who will fight by your side. A partner is a person who cares enough about you to tell you the truth even when it is unpleasant and who doesn't get mad at you or fall out with you just because you're having a bad day! A partner is someone who shares a common vision with you. If this sounds like the definition of a friend, that is no accident. Quite often, the people we partner with become some of our closest and dearest friends. There is something about common experiences and working together on a common cause that binds people together on more than just a superficial level.

Partnerships are powerful. We have more strength and can accomplish much more working in partnership than we could ever do on our on, and in partnership we can encourage and lift up one another. It says in Ecclesiastes, "Two are better than one; because they have a good reward for their labor. For if they fall, the one will lift up his fellow: but woe to him that is alone when he falleth; for he hath not another to help him up....And if one prevail against him, two shall withstand him; and a threefold cord is not quickly broken" (Eccles. 4:9-10, 12). Jesus said, "If two of you shall agree on earth as touching any thing that they shall ask, it shall be done for them of my Father which is in heaven" (Matt. 18:19).

We all need to get plugged into the power of partnership. Any relationship God calls us into will be mutually beneficial. As we begin to partner with other believers we will discover that the anointing of God will increase on our lives and we will find strength beyond ourselves to do what God has laid on our hearts to do. Because we each have the Spirit of God residing in us, whenever we partner together with each other, we are also partnering with God. That is *true* partnership power!

Understand How to be Enabled by Excellence

Finally, if we hope to become image changers in our world, we must understand how to be enabled by excellence. The Bible says that Daniel had an excellent spirit and that spirit resulted in his elevation to the highest position of leadership in Babylon, second only to the king himself. Excellence is a spirit, an anointing from God, because it is possible to do something well and still not do it with excellence. Excellence is more than just doing something right or well; it also involves the attitude—the spirit—in which it is done.

The world is never moved by mediocre people. Although the world is designed to facilitate mediocre people (since the majority of people in the world fit that definition) mediocre people rarely if ever transform their own lives, much less the world. Take an inventory of the movers and shakers of the world and you will find that almost every one is or was a person of excellence, passion, and vision and unwilling to settle for the ordinary and mundane.

Legendary Notre Dame football coach Vince Lombardi once said that winning is a habit, and so is losing, and that the only difference is that winners understand that. The Church needs to have that same understanding. We must train ourselves to think and act like winners, which the Word of God says we already are. Our outcome is assured—we're on the winning team—so we need to live that way.

Christ's call to discipleship is also a call to pursue excellence in every area of life. As our Lord, He is worthy of our very best; in fact, He insists on it. Jesus commands us to give Him first place in our lives. This means that our best is reserved for Him. Remember that Daniel, Shadrach, Meshach and Abednego refused to pollute themselves with the king's meat and wine, choosing to keep themselves pure and holy for the God they loved and served. When examined later, they were found to be ten times better than all the other men being prepared for service in the king's court. By reserving themselves for God, they pursued excellence in His name and proved to be better than anyone serving the secular culture.

A call to pursue excellence does not mean we should strive to be better than anybody else, as much as it means we should seek to be and do our very best in everything we undertake. If we want to change the image of the Church in the eyes of the popular culture, second-best is unacceptable. Anything less than our highest and best effort simply will not do. Christians should be the sharpest thinkers, the hardest workers, the best writers, the most creative artists, the most trustworthy employees, the most principled businesspeople, and the most skilled professionals of any in society.

As with anything else, when it comes to excellence the church should be the leader and not the follower. The ancient Jews knew that only the very best they had was acceptable as an offering to God. A sacrificial lamb had to be perfect and unblemished, the very best of the flock. The tithe, which represented not only the first 10% but also the best of the harvest, belonged to the Lord. God demanded and expected their best.

It is the same way for us. We should settle for nothing less than giving God our very best and seeking to become all that we can be. Part of being a disciple means working to fulfill our fullest potential. Isaiah 60:1 says, "Arise, shine; for thy light is come, and the glory of the Lord is risen upon thee." We have a call to go above and beyond because of the "exceeding greatness of His power" that works inside us (Eph. 1:19). John assures us that "greater is He that is in [us] than he that is in the world" (1 John 4:4) while Paul states that God "is able to do exceeding abundantly above all that we ask or think, according to the power that worketh in us" (Eph. 3:20).

Paul says in Romans that "in all these things we are more than conquerors through him that loved us" (Rom. 8:37) and that "they which receive abundance of grace and the gift of righteousness shall reign in life by one, Jesus Christ" (Rom. 5:17). These promises are not just for the future but also and especially for the here and now. Psalm 118:24 says, "This is the day which the Lord hath made; we will rejoice and be glad in it." Second Corinthians 6:2 says that today is the acceptable time of the Lord; "now is the day of salvation."

And although the "Nebuchadnezzars" of this world try to build and maintain a false image of the Church as the place for losers and has-beens, it is time for the people of God to stand up and tear down that image by the power of God within us and show the world who we really are: children of the King with a calling and a destiny to exercise dominion as stewards of the earth; a people who value and demonstrate excellence in all things. We are the body of Christ and the temple of God, and He wants to shine through us, as treasure in earthen vessels, so that the world will see Him and know He is God. Through us He wants to expose Nebuchadnezzar's false image for what it is so that the people of the world will be set free from the captivity of their negative strongholds and turn to the truth.

This is the power that we have. We are the hands of Jesus. We are the mouth of Jesus. We are the voice of Jesus in the earth. We are the body of Christ, and He has empowered us to fulfill our purpose of bringing down the false image that has been erected against us by the powers that seek to captivate us as well as the rest of the world. In its place will shine not an image of the truth but Truth Himself. Jesus Christ will shine in and through our lives as the Light of the world to those in darkness and as the Truth that can set them free.

SECTION THREE

Power Transfer

Power is moving at all times and discerning people can shift it.

Chapter Six

Culture Shift

One of the most incredible truths in the world is that Christ has given us—everyone who believes in Him through repentance and faith—the power to transform our cities, our communities, and our culture. Perhaps it is more accurate to say that He has afforded us the wonderful privilege of partnering with Him in that transformation. As we willingly surrender our will to His and obey Him as Lord, He channels His power through us to bring about change in our culture and in the lives of those around us.

This power is not reserved only for pastors, career missionaries, or other "professional" ministers; it is the province of *all* believers. Jesus said that we are the "salt of the earth." Salt adds flavor and is also a preservative. The Church is to function in both capacities in society. First, we are to add the wonderful flavor of the gospel of Christ to the world's bland diet of human philosophy and man-made religions that neither nourish nor satisfy. Second, our "salty" presence should help preserve society from judgment and self-destruction so that people can be transformed through the life-giving power of Christ.

Jesus also said that we are the "light of the world." We are to be like a city set on a hill or a candle placed on a candlestick whose light cannot be hidden. Of course, we have no light of our own, but His light—the brightness of Him who is *the* Light of the world—shines in and through us to illuminate the spiritual darkness around us. The apostle Paul described it this way:

> *6For God, who commanded the light to shine out of darkness, hath shined in our hearts, to give the light of the knowledge of the glory of God in the face of Jesus Christ. 7But we have this treasure in earthen vessels, that the excellency of the power may be of God, and not of us* (2 Corinthians 4:6-7).

The Church should shine brightly, a distinctive and compelling presence before the world. Wherever the people of God go, transformation should follow. Anywhere we plant our feet should be different because we were there.

Why then do we see so little transformation of our culture? Why is it that after more than 200 years of religious freedom and Bible preaching and teaching in this country that our cities have not been transformed? How can it be that in a nation with a church on practically every corner, a nation where 80% or more of its citizens claim to believe in God, it is perfectly legal to kill unborn babies in the womb, sexual immorality and perversion abound, and we are still debating whether or not it is "right" to have prayer in the schools or to post the Ten Commandments or a nativity scene on public property?

Why don't we see more spiritual transformation in our cities and towns? One reason is because of the "church culture" that we have allowed to develop and that we have participated in, a church culture that has "a form of godliness, but denying the power thereof" (2 Tim. 3:5), a dry shell that sucks the life and the divine revelation right out of the air. In America today we have as much empty religion as we do genuine relationship with God; as much form and ritual as we do power and demonstration.

By and large, we do not see transformation because we lack the power for transformation. Why do we lack the power? Because we look to our own wisdom, our own resources, and our own understanding instead of looking to God.

Listen to the wisdom of Proverbs:

> *5 Trust in the Lord with all thine heart; and lean not unto thine own understanding. 6 In all thy ways acknowledge him, and he shall direct thy paths* (Proverbs 3:5-6).

Wisdom says we should trust in the Lord with all our heart and *lean not on our own understanding.* I believe that is where our problem lies. We have an entire generation of people in the Church (maybe more) who think that everything should fit according to their own understanding. If something doesn't make sense (so goes their reasoning) then it simply can't be right. Unless they can know everything up front or work everything out in advance, they want no part of it.

Isaiah 55:8-9 says that God's thoughts and ways not only are different from ours but also higher than ours. God does not think or act the way we do. His thoughts and ways are beyond our comprehension, which is why we can know nothing of them unless God reveals them to us. As long as we lean (trust) in our own understanding, we will never understand God's ways.

What does this mean in practical terms? Our natural tendency in any area—health, finances, general decision making—is to look first toward human wisdom and man-made solutions. For example, despite the many scriptural references on how to be happy and filled with joy, many believers, if diagnosed with depression, will automatically turn to medication as a *first* resort. I'm not denying the value and importance of modern medicine or discouraging anyone from seeking appropriate treatment. What I am saying is that such an automatic recourse to medicine often reflects a tacit assumption that no solution is possible from God. Couples struggling with financial problems look to the bank for help instead of the Bible. Far too often in the problems and affairs of everyday life, looking to God for the answer is our *last* resort, the option we try when all of *our* solutions have failed.

The key to supernatural transforming power in life as well as in church is learning to appreciate the resources we have without relying on them. God is our source, and He is the One on whom we should depend. No matter how much He may have given us, we cannot lean on what we have. We cannot lean on our money. We cannot lean on our intelligence, wisdom, knowledge, or education. We cannot lean on our building to attract people. We cannot lean on our talent to move people. We cannot lean on our organization to transform people. We must learn to trust in the Lord and lean on Him alone.

When we keep everything in proper perspective, doing what we can with our resources while trusting the Lord for the rest, He will do the things that we cannot do. He will deliver the bound and the oppressed. He will heal those who need healing and save those who need saving. He will impart new life to those who trust in Him. If we trust in the Lord, He will transform us and through us transform our cities and our culture.

Transforming Our Church Culture

Before we can have any real hope of transforming the greater culture we live in, we must first transform our church culture. Many churches in America today are so steeped in a culture of powerlessness, accommodation, and compromise that they have marginalized themselves and lost touch completely with both the heartbeat and the heart cry of the people they should be reaching for Christ. Some may be locked in tradition that no longer has any real meaning or relevance while others espouse faulty theology and doctrine that effectively strip them of any true spiritual authority. Whatever the case, the end result is a dead church culture that has no power to change anything and that offers nothing that contemporary Americans feel they either need or want.

We need to build a church culture that carries the power to transform our communities. What would such a church culture look like? I want to share with you ten characteristics that I believe every church needs if it wants to reach people and transform lives through the power of the gospel of Christ. These are the same characteristics that we have set in place and are constantly building in our church in Toledo and I recommend them to you and your church without hesitation or reservation.

1. A church culture of *forward thinking* people. Many churches are consistently twenty years behind everybody else. Their music is outdated and in structure and theology they are always trying to reach back into yesterday to prop up something that was. Some churches are so backward-thinking that walking into them is like stepping into a time machine. If the Church is to be relevant, we must keep up with the times. This does not mean compromising our witness, diluting the gospel message, or sacrificing our Christian moral and spiritual values. It does mean finding new and fresh ways to present the timeless truths of our faith to each new generation. Jesus said that the children of this world are wiser in their generation than are the children of light. This should not be so. The Church must be forward in its thinking. We must be innovative and ahead of the curve; pace-setters who are always moving forward and never afraid to try new things if they will reach people for Christ.

2. A church culture of *manifestation without weirdness*. This means a church culture that believes in the full gospel—all the miracles, all the signs and wonders, the whole power of God to save, heal and deliver, all of the Bible from Genesis through Revelation—yet resists the mentality that says believing these things has to make us "flaky." The Spirit of God can speak into our hearts at any time and in any place without us going "weird" to the people around us. He can direct our paths without our putting on a scary display of strange behavior as if we just stepped off the "mother ship."

Some churches seek and welcome manifestation but don't understand how to bring it into balance with everything else. As a result, these churches end up filled with weird, "subjective revelation" people who cannot be pastored because they place all of their visions and feelings and angelic visitations and goose bumps and the like on an equal footing with the Word of God.

Manifestation without weirdness means that we measure and judge all such experiences against the standard of God's Word. Whatever measures up we embrace; whatever doesn't, we don't. There is more than enough manifestation with the real thing; we don't have to make anything up. Just stick around God long enough and we'll see miracles; we'll see signs; we'll see wonders because God is a wonder worker. But He can also do all of these things in and through us without making us behave in a weird or strange manner.

3. A church culture of *punctuality*. Punctuality simply means being on time. This may sound trivial at first until we understand that many times the Church is unable to reach its communities because in the eyes of the world church people are notorious for being late, last, and lost. The Church is the visible embodiment of the Kingdom of God; the city set on a hill; the light of the world. Our calling is to let our light so shine before men that they see our good works and glorify our Father in heaven. What kind of example do we set if the world sees the people of God as perpetually a day late and a dollar short? What does that say about us? More importantly, what does it tell them about the God we serve?

Being late all the time communicates the message that we place little importance on what we do. We don't care enough even to show up on time! Think of all the church folks you know who consistently come traipsing in 15, 20, or even 30 minutes after the service starts. What would happen if we acted that way on our jobs? What would happen if our kids were always late for sports practice or music lessons? Punctuality at church shows that we consider what God is doing important enough to show up where we're supposed to be, when we're supposed to be there.

Punctuality is the virtue of princes. As members of the body of Christ, we are also members of God's royal family, so punctuality should be among our virtues. Punctuality says that our time is important and also that other people's time is important. By striving to be punctual we acknowledge that we each are in charge of our own time and that authority begins with ourselves and our alarm clocks. Punctuality is a sign of maturity and responsibility. When we are punctual as a way of life, we honor God.

4. A church culture of *participatory services*. A church worship service is not a spectator sport; it is an audience participation event! In fact, worship has been compared to a theatrical production in which God is the audience, the worship leaders are the "prompters," and the worshippers are the actors. Too many Christians come to church and sit in the pew, never moving a muscle, with an expression on their face that says, "Okay, entertain me." Worship is not entertainment (although it should be fun and joyful); it calls for active involvement and participation.

Participatory services are important because we get out of something no more than we invest in it. The Bible itself is a participatory book. Throughout Scripture we see God and His people actively participating with each other: God working in and through His people delivering them, defeating their enemies, and confirming His Word with signs following. Jesus called His followers to a life of discipleship, a participatory lifestyle of faithfulness and obedience. This kind of life calls for the practice of active learning in which the learners are as active as the teacher.

True worship is participatory because it engages all our senses; it draws us in body, heart and soul. Paul stated it this way: "I will pray with the spirit, and I will pray with the understanding also: I will sing with the spirit, and I will sing with the understanding also" (1 Cor. 14:15). That means we've got to put our hearts and minds in gear and get involved. The more we participate, the more God works in us. As Phil Pringle once said, "God moves in our moving." God is not only to be studied; He is also to be experienced. In order to experience Him, we must get involved with Him. The only way to experience

God or receive anything from Him is to participate actively in the process.

5. A church culture of *acceptance that releases freedom.* The Church should be a place where anyone can find unconditional love and acceptance. This means that the Church must be free of bigotry, racism, legalism, denominationalism, and any other "ism" or attitude that prejudges people. Acceptance frees people to be who they are, as well as to become the people God is making them into. Second Corinthians 3:17 says, "Where the Spirit of the Lord is, there is liberty." Although this verse certainly means that the Spirit of God gives freedom from bondages, addictions, and destructive lifestyles, the actual context of the verse refers to freedom from legalism; freedom from religious systems of do's and don'ts, of touch not, taste not and handle not.

Nurturing an atmosphere of acceptance does not mean permissive love or coddling people in their sin. Neither does it mean lowering our moral or ethical standards. There are times when we must confront and challenge someone who is wrong, but an atmosphere of acceptance assures that such a confrontation is done in love and from a genuine desire to see the other person made whole. We must be careful to keep ourselves and our churches free of all impurity and immorality. At the same time, however, we cannot help people if we do not have an atmosphere of acceptance that says, "Come into God's house and find deliverance. Come into God's house and find life." Our goal is not to change people into our image of who they should be but to bring them into the presence of God where the Holy Spirit can change them into the image of Christ.

6. A church culture that *embraces order.* The apostle Paul said, "God is not the author of confusion, but of peace" (1 Cor.

14:33). Any church that wants to become a transforming power in its community must resist the mentality that says God has to have a chaotic atmosphere before He can move. God is a God of order. He sets up rank and authority and measure. Order does not mean boring or restrained. It simply means doing the right thing at the right time in the right way. Because God is orderly, it is possible for us to welcome a strong moving of His Spirit and still embrace order. In fact, disorderly proceedings are a clue that the Spirit of God is *not* in control. We must be open to the Spirit but also careful to ensure that everything is done "decently and in order" (1 Cor. 14:40).

7. A church culture that embraces *increase with integrity.* God's people ought to increase. The Church ought to prosper. I'm not talking about a gospel of *excess* but a gospel of *success.* God said that He wants His people to prosper. After all, the first command He gave to man was to be fruitful and multiply and fill and subdue the earth. Our original mandate from God was a mandate of prosperity and success, and God has never rescinded it. God doesn't get any glory out of broken, beaten down poor people who can't feed their kids or churches that can't pay their bills. He wants us to succeed.

The gospel of Jesus Christ is a gospel of success, of triumph, of victory. God told Joshua that if He meditated on the law daily and obeyed it faithfully, he would have "good success" (Josh. 1:8). First John 4:4 assures us that He who is in us is greater than he that is in the world. Deuteronomy 8:18 says that it is God who gives us power to get wealth. The earth is the Lord's and everything in it (Ps. 24:1). He owns all the gold and silver and the "cattle upon a thousand hills" (Ps. 50:10). God delights in the prosperity of His servants. Our God is a prospering God, a blessing God, a God of increase.

Increase with integrity means being responsible and honorable with the wealth and assets God blesses us with. It means understanding that God did not call us just to be wage earners but asset owners. He didn't call us to live from paycheck to paycheck but to invest our paycheck as our "seed" to get a profitable return. It means being committed to pulling our own weight, paying our own way, and not expecting breaks or deals just because we're Christians. It means paying our bills on time and developing a reputation as the most trustworthy folks in town when it comes to money. It means always treating people well and using every opportunity to bless others as we have been blessed.

8. A church culture that is *generationally minded.* This means understanding that although we are called to serve the purposes of God for our generation, we are also responsible for preparing the next generation. Many churches are ineffective in making a difference in their culture because they plan only for the season they are in and not for the future. Being generationally-minded means understanding that what we do not accomplish, our children will accomplish because we will put them on our shoulders and launch them into the next generation.

We do this by instilling in them the truth that success is within their grasp because God has designed them to prosper. People rise to the level of the culture they are in. For this reason, we surround our children with excellence in example, teaching, facilities, supplies, and equipment. Many churches force their children to make do with substandard teaching, supplies, and facilities and then wonder why the children don't believe it when they are told that God wants to use them to win the world.

The Church's resources for training the next generation should be superior to anything available in the secular culture, including the public schools. We cannot give our children sub-standard ministry in substandard facilities and expect the gospel to increase. We must show them that the Christian faith is not a hobby but relates to the very purpose of life itself. Let's surround our children with excellence. They deserve our very best. When we do what we can do, God will do what we cannot do! If we learn to lean not on our own understanding and ability, but trust in God, He will put an anointing in the classroom and our children will receive something on Sundays that will shift everything they hear the rest of the week.

9. A church culture of *identifiable leadership*. This characteristic is closely related to the characteristic of order in the Church. Few things are more potentially destructive to healthy church life than confusion in leadership. Without clearly defined leadership, visitors to the church, whether nonbelievers, new believers, or anyone else, won't know who to listen to and can easily fall prey to every self-appointed prophet, evangelist, or missionary who wants to share with them a "word from the Lord." When people don't know who to listen to, they listen to everybody.

Knowing who to listen to is almost as important as knowing what to listen to because the quality of the teaching depends on the quality of the teacher and the soundness of the leadership depends on the soundness of the leader. The apostle Paul said that we should "know them which labor among you, and are over you in the Lord, and admonish you, and...esteem them highly in love for their work's sake" (1 Thess. 5:12-13).

Trained, approved, appointed, trustworthy and clearly identifiable leaders eliminate confusion and protect the body of Christ and the reputation of His name by helping to assure that no erroneous teachings, half-baked ideas or misguided projects are released to wreak havoc either in the church fellowship or the greater community.

10. A church culture of *ministering members*. Ministry is not reserved for the "professional" clergy or the spiritual elite. Every Christian is a minister, which means that every Christian has a ministry. We all have something of value to add. Some people's ministry is in the church while others minister in the community as coaches, teachers, tutors, business professionals, volunteers, health care professionals, law enforcement personnel, bus drivers, and mechanics. Some work in hospices or in unwed mothers' homes while others work in community service. Virtually any type of legal and moral work or occupation can be a ministry when done for the glory and honor of the Lord.

Jesus said, "It is more blessed to give than to receive" (Acts 20:35). In order to be fulfilled in life, we all must find something to do that takes us out of ourselves, something for which the only reward we receive is the joy that comes in serving others. As we minister in Jesus' name—no matter what form our ministry takes—His light shines through us and the world sees Him. That is what Jesus meant when He said, "Let your light so shine before men, that they may see your good works, and glorify your Father which is in heaven" (Matt. 5:16).

One of the reasons that people don't turn and glorify our Father in heaven is because when they look at us they hear a lot of talk but see no works. We are the salt of the earth and the light of the world. A culture-transforming church is made up of ministering members who understand that the world will never be changed until every believer gets out of the pew and steps onto the frontline.

Transforming Our City

It takes the right kind of church culture to transform a community, but how does that transformation occur? What process goes on to bring it about? Cultural change does not occur overnight. Like a garden being readied for spring planting, the spiritual "soil" of society must be prepared in order for any transformation to become widespread and permanent. One picture of this process is found in the seventh chapter of Second Kings in a story relating how the Word of the Lord transformed Samaria, the capital city of the Northern Kingdom of Israel. Samaria was under siege by the Syrians and the people were facing famine. God was about to bring deliverance. The account begins with a confrontation between the great prophet Elisha and one of the king's aides.

> *¹Then Elisha said, Hear ye the word of the Lord; Thus saith the Lord, Tomorrow about this time shall a measure of fine flour be sold for a shekel, and two measures of barley for a shekel, in the gate of Samaria. ²Then a lord on whose hand the king leaned answered the man of God, and said, Behold, if the Lord would make windows in heaven, might this thing be? And he said, Behold, thou shalt see it with thine eyes, but shalt not eat thereof.*
>
> *³And there were four leprous men at the entering in of the gate: and they said one to another, Why sit we here until we die? ⁴If we say, We will enter into the city, then the famine is in the city, and we shall die there: and if we sit still here, we die also. Now therefore come, and let us fall unto the host of the Syrians: if they save us alive, we shall live; and if they kill us, we shall but die. ⁵And they rose up in the twilight, to go unto the camp of the Syrians: and when they were come to the uttermost part of the camp of Syria, behold, there was no man there. ⁶For the Lord had made the host of the Syrians to hear a noise of chariots, and a noise of horses, even the*

noise of a great host: and they said one to another, Lo, the king of Israel hath hired against us the kings of the Hittites, and the kings of the Egyptians, to come upon us. ⁷Wherefore they arose and fled in the twilight, and left their tents, and their horses, and their asses, even the camp as it was, and fled for their life. ⁸And when these lepers came to the uttermost part of the camp, they went into one tent, and did eat and drink, and carried thence silver, and gold, and raiment, and went and hid it; and came again, and entered into another tent, and carried thence also, and went and hid it. ⁹Then they said one to another, We do not well: this day is a day of good tidings, and we hold our peace: if we tarry till the morning light, some mischief will come upon us: now therefore come, that we may go and tell the king's household. ¹⁰So they came and called unto the porter of the city: and they told them, saying, We came to the camp of the Syrians, and, behold, there was no man there, neither voice of man, but horses tied, and asses tied, and the tents as they were. ¹¹And he called the porters; and they told it to the king's house within (2 Kings 7:1-11).

Suspecting a Syrian trap, the king of Israel sent messengers out to scout out the enemy camp and report back. Finding things exactly as the four lepers had said, the messengers rode as far as the Jordan, seeing along the way clothing and equipment that the Syrians had discarded in their haste to get away. Quickly, they returned to the king with this good news.

¹⁶And the people went out, and spoiled the tents of the Syrians. So a measure of fine flour was sold for a shekel, and two measures of barley for a shekel, according to the word of the Lord. ¹⁷And the king appointed the lord

*on whose hand he leaned to have the charge of the gate:
and the people trode upon him in the gate, and he died,
as the man of God had said, who spake when the king
came down to him. [18]And it came to pass as the man
of God had spoken to the king, saying, Two measures
of barley for a shekel, and a measure of fine flour for a
shekel, shall be tomorrow about this time in the gate of
Samaria* (2 Kings 7:16-18).

God had a word of deliverance for the king and people
of Samaria but before it could take root, the soil had to be prepared. The atmosphere had to be changed before the people
would be ready to believe and embrace a new reality. Looking
more closely at this passage we can identify seven steps in this
process of preparing the city for transformation.

1. Crisis

First of all, Samaria was facing crisis. The city was in survival mode. Famine was spreading and the people were in danger of starving. One of the dangers of famine is that if people
get hungry enough, they'll eat anything. Several other accounts
in the Old Testament describe famine so severe that people even
resorted to eating their own children.

Like the starving citizens of Samaria, there are people in
our culture who are so starved for truth that they will gobble up
any idea or truth-claim message that seems even remotely plau-
sible. Modern purveyors of falsehood are sly, disguising their
lies and demonic doctrines by changing their terminology and
dropping their labels in order to entrap new ranks of the hungry
and the gullible.

Under their new guise, many of these false messages have
adopted biblical terminology and migrated from the "New Age,"

"Occult," and "Metaphysical" sections of bookstores to the "Religious" section. Many people, including far too many Christians, don't know the Bible well enough to see past the terminology and discern a "new age" doctrine from a biblical doctrine. They are so indoctrinated with secular humanism that their minds are clouded to the truths of God's Word.

Most people don't know what they believe because they have no solid foundation. They are so hungry for validation that without a strong church culture to help them develop a stable belief system they will run after anything. People are hungry for miracles. They're hungry for their families to be put back together. They're hungry for self-esteem. They're hungry for a philosophy of life that actually works. They're hungry to know that God is real and loves them. They're hungry but don't know what to eat.

Like ancient Samaria, our cities today are in crisis. Spiritual famine is starving the souls of millions of Americans and they are scrabbling for every morsel of hope and meaning they can get their hands on. Our cities are ripe for transformation. The good thing about crisis is that God often uses it to set the stage for divine reversal. Spiritual famine often becomes the catalyst that brings the Word of the Lord to the forefront.

2. Questions

Sustained crisis leads to questions: "What's wrong?" "Why is this happening?" "What am I missing?" Asking questions is the beginning stage of a movement. Plato said that the unexamined life is not worth living. Martin Luther King, Jr. stated that one of the signs of maturity is the ability to be self-critical. Questions provoke the search for answers and answers bring knowledge and illumination. A person who walks through life without any questions is a person who is blind on the journey.

155

Outside Samaria's gate, four leprous men unknowingly set the city on its way to transformation. It began with a question. The crisis had reached such a proportion that finally one of the men asked, "Why sit we here until we die?" Questioning is key to change because nothing will ever change until somebody questions the status quo. Our finances will never change until we question our financial condition. Our families will never change or be restored until we question what is wrong. Our churches will never become power shifters until we question our lack of effectiveness.

Regarding the crisis in our cities today, many people in our nation consider the Church to be part of the problem. On the contrary, the Church is (or should be) the answer! One of the reasons the Church fails to change our cities is because the Church is one of the few institutions in the world that refuses to question its own behavior! We don't question why we tolerate silliness, weirdness, and error. We don't question why our members don't tithe. We don't question why we refuse to change. We don't question why we do what we do. Lack of introspection leads to stagnation and slow death. If the Church dies, there is no solid food to satisfy the spiritual famine that is rampant in the land. Someone needs to start asking, "Why sit we here until we die?"

3. Options

Questions illuminate options. Once people begin questioning the status quo, they start looking for alternatives. Why do people stay in abusive relationships or dead-end jobs year after year? Many times it's because they don't realize they have options. Why do so many churches refuse to change and continue doing things that are ineffective even as they watch their membership dwindle away? Someone said that the seven last words of the church are, "We never did it that way before." Churches don't change because they don't realize they have options. How could they if they never ask the questions that lead to options?

Crisis led the four lepers outside Samaria to consider their options. First, if they stayed where they were, they would die. Second, they could go into the city where the famine raged and die there. Since they were dying anyway, at least in the city they would die in a better place. Third, they could go over to the Syrians, who might kill them, in which case they would be no worse off than they already were. In fact, a quick death at the hands of the Syrians would be better than a slow death by starvation. On the other hand (fourth), the Syrians might spare their lives and even perhaps give them food. They chose to go to the Syrian camp. It seemed the most promising option.

Even in the church culture there are options. We each have the option to choose what kind of Christian we will be, whether a victimized, barely get through, tie-a-knot-in-the-rope-and-hang-on kind of a Christian or an overcoming, forward-thinking, asset-owning Christian who is ready to move out and possess the land. Our choice will help determine the character of our church, which will determine whether or not our church can be a power shifter in the culture.

4. Risk

Options open the door to risk. This is because options reveal the possibility for change and change is always risky. Choosing and following an option is a courageous act because it is risky and taking a risk requires courage. Risk implies the potential to fail. Sometimes it is worth risking failure to get something we can't get without risk. The four lepers said, "If we go to the Syrians, they may kill us; then again, maybe they won't. If we stay here we will surely die but if we go there we may die and we may not. It's worth the risk. After all, what have we got to lose?"

It is always amazing to see people who don't have anything to lose act as though they do. When you have nothing to lose, *go ahead and risk it!* Suppose you have been financially unstable for years but won't risk tithing. What have you got to lose? You're already broke. Risk it! Step out on faith and God just might turn your situation around. Suppose your life is falling apart or you are bound up with an addiction. You go to church and the Holy Spirit convicts you that you need Jesus. Somebody comes up to you and says, "Give Jesus a chance," and you reply, "Oh, I don't know." What are you waiting for? What have you got to lose? Risk it! Step out on faith and embrace Jesus. Martyred missionary Jim Elliott said, "He is no fool who gives what he cannot keep to gain what he cannot lose." If you have nothing to lose, you also have nothing to hold onto, so risk it! You just may find that you gain everything.

Change always involves risk. No great accomplishment ever happens without risk! Somebody has to step out of the boat! Somebody has to throw a rock at the giant! Somebody has to say: "Why sit we here until we die? Let's risk it. We've got nothing to lose and maybe a lot to gain. Let's make a change."

Risk. We'll never change our culture without it.

5. Action

Risk brings people to the point of action. Action is just another way of saying, "Do something!" Nothing will ever change until we take action. The four lepers could have debated their options all day but in the end they would have been in the same hopeless situation. Instead, they acted on their option. They took the risk and started walking toward the Syrian camp. The

Bible says it was twilight when they began. Not only did they take a risky action, but they did it at night! Once they decided to move they didn't wait around.

Have you ever noticed that when the anointing is on you to do something, if you wait to act until the anointing lifts, you don't want to do it anymore? Suppose you are in a time of prayer, broken before the Lord, and you say, "Lord, I'll do anything you ask!" And the Lord replies, "Then call your friend or family member and apologize for the hateful things you said to them." The anointing is on you and you say, "Yes, Lord." If you don't act immediately, you're liable to start thinking about it and put it off. Before long the anointing will lift, and that's when you remember *why* you said those things to your friend. They made you angry and hurt your feelings. Now, instead of obeying the Lord, you start justifying why *you* shouldn't apologize. "They should come to me!" Now, suddenly, you're mad at them all over again.

Here's the point: even when we know what to do, nothing will change until we do it. An option is no good unless we act on it.

6. Open Door

Action reveals an open door. Until we take action, we will never know what unexpected opportunity or blessing awaits us. The four lepers approached the Syrian camp expecting to be captured and perhaps killed. Instead, they discovered that God had routed the Syrians during the night by causing them to hear sounds that led them to think they were about to be attacked by a superior force. They fled, leaving everything behind. The four lepers apparently heard nothing. Why not? Because they were walking in faith. They simply walked into the empty Syrian camp and helped themselves to the spoils of their nation's enemy.

As Christians, we walk by faith and not by sight (2 Cor. 5:7). When God wants to increase our faith, He may decrease our sight for a time so that we learn to trust in Him rather than lean on our own understanding. Something may seem impossible to us, but when we step out in faith we find that God has opened wide the door and all we have to do is walk through it into transformed circumstances.

7. Increase

An open door leads to increase. This is the final step in the process. The people who had nothing—the four lepers—suddenly walked into a place of abundance and increase. Donkeys were still tied up. Horses were still in the stables. Food was still cooking in the pots. Gold, silver and precious gems were abandoned in the tents. Those four men simply helped themselves. It was a true "rags to riches" story.

The last step before a city is transformed is when God places increase into the hands of faithful stewards who are willing to risk everything to effect change in their culture in His name. God's increase is not to be hoarded, however, but shared openly so that everyone can be blessed. After a night of enriching themselves with the spoils of the Syrians and celebrating their bounty, one of the four lepers said, "This is a day of good news, and here we are keeping it to ourselves. That's not right. We need to go back to the city and tell everybody." So that's what they did.

Ironically, the king thought it was a Syrian trap. He suspected that when the people entered the Syrian camp, the Syrians would rise up out of hiding and ambush them. Once the people discovered that what the lepers said was true, they tore the gates down trying to get into the place!

The king's suspicion is the same attitude with which many people in our culture today approach the Church. They think something bad will happen just from walking through the door. That's how the enemy works with people's minds. But like the news the lepers took back to their city, the gospel of Jesus Christ is "good news" for ours. If we can develop the right kind of church culture by which the world can see that the Church consists of believers who are not flaky or flashy or phony, but stable, solid people who know and live the truth that can transform lives, people from the secular culture will tear the doors down trying to get into the Church.

People are hungry for truth and when they see it lived out in a practical and powerful way, they will flock to become part of it. That's the way to transform our cities.

We are living in incredible days, days where we cannot afford to get wrapped up in simply living our lives while God's purpose passes us by. Now is the acceptable time! Today is the day of salvation! We are in the season of the favor of God. It's time for us to trust God. It's time for us to take the limits off God and believe that He can do whatever He says He will do. It's time for us to believe that God can and will use us to transform our cities, our culture, and our nation. It's time for a *power transfer!*

Cultural transformation involves a
God-initiated power shift from the secular
culture to the kingdom culture.

Chapter Seven

Power Transfer

Before a church can become a transforming agent in its community, it has to build the kind of church culture that will produce Christians who can handle the power transfer involved. It's not a question of who loves God the most or who God loves the most, but a question of who is willing to be a catalyst for change by becoming a conduit of God's transforming power.

Not every Christian is ready for such a challenge, either by teaching or by temperament. Different kinds of church cultures produce different kinds of Christians. Some produce victimized, woe-is-me, "circle-the-wagons" kind of Christians who are just trying to hang on until Jesus comes back. Others produce dynamic, power-shifting, take-the-world-for-Jesus kind of Christians who know that the earth belongs to the Lord, not the devil, that the wealth of the wicked is being laid up for the righteous, and that the church has the divine calling and authority to engage and transform the secular culture through the power of the gospel of Jesus Christ. The first group withdraws from the culture while the second advances toward it with boldness.

Cultural transformation involves a God-initiated power shift from the secular culture to the Kingdom culture. It is this second group of Christians who are prepared to be conduits of the necessary power transfer. They are the city-set-on-a-hill, light-in-dark-places, dominion-minded believers. While others play games in the marketplace of ideas and philosophies, these have come to transact serious business.

God is always looking for people to whom He can transfer power. Who do you think He will entrust that power to, those who want to play games or those who will take His business seriously? Consider the words of Jesus:

> *[16]But whereunto shall I liken this generation? It is like unto children sitting in the markets, and calling unto their fellows, [17]And saying, We have piped unto you, and ye have not danced; we have mourned unto you, and ye have not lamented. [18]For John came neither eating nor drinking, and they say, He hath a devil. [19]The Son of man came eating and drinking, and they say, Behold a man gluttonous, and a winebibber, a friend of publicans and sinners. But wisdom is justified of her children* (Matthew 11:16-19).

The phrase "wisdom is justified of her children" means that the fruit of something is the evidence of whether or not that something is wisdom or foolishness. In other words, if you want to know the true character or nature of something, look at what it produces. A good tree produces good fruit and a bad tree produces bad fruit. Wisdom begets wisdom and folly begets folly.

Jesus likened His generation (and it applies to ours also) to "children sitting in the markets." His comparison refers not to chronology but to behavior. The marketplace was a place of business but children would come there to play while their parents shopped. Jesus said, in effect, that the grownups of that generation behaved like children in the marketplace, playing when they should be taking care of business.

The marketplace is the place of transaction, the place where power is being shifted. Transaction means to move something from one place to another. Children in the marketplace are in the place of power, where power is being shifted, but because they are children, they are unaware of where they are. While power is being shifted, while currency is moving, while transactions are being made, they are busy playing.

To what shall we liken this church generation? Many people have been brought into the Kingdom of God and have been put in a place where transaction is happening, but they are too busy "playing church" to realize that all around them power is shifting. Wisdom is justified of her children. Wisdom brings us to the place where we realize that things are shifting around us and we are in the position to grab hold of transaction of power, a transfer of wealth through the moving of the power of God. As long as we remain unaware of the transactions occurring around us, we are like the child in a marketplace who runs through the sale racks while Momma's trying on clothes. Certain church cultures produce certain kinds of Christians.

It is very important for us to understand that we cannot reach the world with the kind of Christians that many of our churches are growing. Countless believers sit inside the walls of the church for years and never get to where they're supposed to go because they never adapt themselves to the culture of the Kingdom of God. Rather than trusting in the Lord they continue to lean on their own understanding.

Wisdom is justified of her children. After twenty years of preaching, when I visit another church I don't have to hear the preacher preach or the congregation sing to know what they teach. All I have to do is talk to a few of the people and I can tell you their theology. I know a victimized Christian when I meet one. An apocalyptic, ready-to-get-out-of-here, no-possessing Christian is easy to identify. I can spot a flaky, "weirdness-manifesting" Christian a mile away. I can also quickly recognize mature, solid, well-grounded disciples of the Lord when I come into contact with them. They are the ones who are confident, enthusiastic, strong in faith, sensitive in spirit, and compassionate of heart; bold visionaries who expect God to do great things in them, through them, and around them.

In our own day there is rising up on the earth a generation of the people of God who will not be as children in the marketplace. They will not sit playing games during a season of transfer while power shifts over their heads. No, they will get involved in the power transfer and grab what God has said is theirs and shift nations and families in the name of Jesus. Are you a part of that generation?

The Equalization of Truth

A power transfer is what occurred in the story of the four leprous men that we looked at in chapter six of Second Kings. Consider how the circumstances changed through the course of the story. In the beginning, the Syrian army had the power. Their long siege of Samaria had left the city on the brink of starvation. The citizens of Samaria, who were Israelites and, therefore, God's people, were virtually powerless. Nevertheless, the prophet Elisha proclaimed, "Thus saith the Lord, Tomorrow about this time shall a measure of fine flour be sold for a shekel, and two measures of barley for a shekel, in the gate of

Samaria" (2 Kings 7:1). In simple terms he said, "In 24 hours the famine will be over." Elisha prophesied that a power transfer would take place that would shift power from the Syrians to the people of God.

Sure enough, the four leprous men walked into a deserted Syrian camp and when they reported their find, the entire city of Samaria celebrated. Beginning with the four lepers, everyone satisfied their hunger with the Syrians' food and enriched themselves with the Syrians' spoils. By the end of the story, power had shifted from the supposedly invincible Syrians to the famished, victimized Israelites, and it started with those four leprous men.

Here's the clincher: *those four lepers did not hear the prophet's words when he spoke them.* They were outside the walls of the city but were sitting at the city gate. In those days of walled cities with traders and merchants going in and out, the city gate was a place where business was transacted. Money and power changed hands at the gate. The four leprous men did not hear Elisha say, "Tomorrow about this time...," but change was already in the air, which prompted them to ask, "Why sit we here until we die?" Spurred by that question, they decided to risk everything, took action and went to the Syrian camp where they found open doors and increase that transformed their city.

Unknowingly, these men acted under a principle known as the *equalization of truth.* The equalization of truth means that just because we may not know when God has released something on the earth does not mean we cannot work with it once it has been released. When God releases a thing, He releases it, and anyone who picks it up can run with it.

How long had those lepers sat there before they questioned their situation? No one knows. It was not until God released His Word through Elisha about the power transfer that the question came to their lips, "Why sit we here until we die?"

Even though they did not *hear* the Lord's Word spoken, when they acted on their question they were working *in line* with the Word that had been spoken. Because when God speaks a word, you can be working with the word that you never even heard.

The equalization of truth means that when God speaks a thing anybody can tap into it, including nonbelievers. When God releases a thing He just releases it and whoever has ears to hear can plug in and reap the increase. The Bible says that man does not live by bread alone but by every word that proceeds out of the mouth of God (Matt. 4:4). What the Bible does *not* say is that everybody in the marketplace is a believer. This does not inhibit their ability to take part in the power shift that God has released. Sometimes secular people who are transacting business benefit from shifts of power and economy while God's people play like children, oblivious to what is happening over their heads. Somebody else is working with the Word that God released because they perceive something, "a change in the air," perhaps, even though they don't know where it came from.

When God speaks a word it becomes the equalization of truth, which means that everybody has equal access to that truth. If everyone has equal access, then anyone in the world can pick up on it. This is not equalization of *thought* but equalization of *truth*. All truth is God's truth, and truth has its own power. When a word's time has come, God releases a word for that time.

Think about this: if you lived in the days of the Egyptian bondage, wouldn't that greatly limit your ability to prosper? Your status as a slave would greatly reduce your options. If you were alive at the time of the Exodus, however, your prospects of prosperity would increase significantly. The Bible says that when Moses led the Israelites out of Egypt, God gave them favor in the eyes of the Egyptians, who showered them with gold and silver and all kinds of precious treasures as they left. God spoke a word of deliverance and power shifted. Just because one person died in bondage and another lived to see freedom does not mean that the first loved God less and the second loved God more. It simply means that each was governed by the words that had been released over the days in which he lived.

On the Day of Pentecost Simon Peter spoke to the crowd in Jerusalem of a Word that God had released over the earth, a Word whose time had come and which is still active in our own day. Quoting from the Book of Joel, Peter said:

> *[17]And it shall come to pass in the last days, saith God, I will pour out of my Spirit upon all flesh: and your sons and your daughters shall prophesy, and your young men shall see visions, and your old men shall dream dreams: [18]And on my servants and on my handmaidens I will pour out in those days of my Spirit; and they shall prophesy* (Acts 2:17-18).

What this means for us is that we are living in a time when there is a power transfer from God to His people.

If we had lived during the 400 years of prophetic silence between Malachi and Matthew, our potential to receive that blessing would have been drastically reduced. There are always exceptions. In every generation, special people with special faith have been able to transcend their age and go into the future, but in general, people's prospects are governed by the word they are under for that time or that generation. Our time is a day in which God has said He will transfer power from His account to our account, a process we call "being filled with the Holy Spirit." Because of the divine Word we live under in our day, the filling of the Holy Spirit is available to every child of God equally; all we have to do is ask. This is the equalization of truth. Power transfer is underway.

The Place of Transfer

Jacob's experience in the wilderness is a good illustration of the transforming power of being in a place of divine transfer. Fleeing from the murderous wrath of his brother Esau, Jacob stopped for the night in a barren place in the wilderness where he had only a rock for a pillow. Settling down to sleep, he never expected to have an encounter with God.

> *12And he dreamed, and behold a ladder set up on the earth, and the top of it reached to heaven: and behold the angels of God ascending and descending on it. 13And, behold, the Lord stood above it, and said, I am the Lord God of Abraham thy father, and the God of Isaac: the land whereon thou liest, to thee will I give it, and to thy seed; 14And thy seed shall be as the dust of the earth, and thou shalt spread abroad to the west, and to the east, and to the north, and to the south: and in thee and in thy seed shall all the families of the earth be blessed. 15And, behold, I am with thee, and will keep thee in all places whither thou goest, and will bring thee again into this land; for I will not leave thee, until I have done that which I have spoken to thee of.*
>
> *16And Jacob awaked out of his sleep, and he said, Surely the Lord is in this place; and I knew it not. 17And he was afraid, and said, How dreadful is this place! This is none other but the house of God, and this is the gate of heaven* (Genesis 28:12-17).

It is possible for God to be doing something and we be asleep to what He is doing. That was Jacob's situation. When he went to sleep he thought he was alone in the desert. His dream revealed otherwise. The Lord appeared to Jacob in his dream and gave him a marvelous promise of future prosperity and fruitfulness that would bless everyone on earth. Is it any wonder that Jacob woke up in complete awe and fear of the Lord?

Look at what Jacob said: "This is none other but the house of God, and this is the gate of heaven." Remember, the gate of a city is where business transactions took place. Jacob recognized the place of his divine encounter as "the house of God" and "the gate of heaven." He was in the place of transaction. The house of God is the place of divine transfer, the place of transformation. Jacob's experience completely transformed his life. He went from being a conniving schemer (which is the meaning of his name, Jacob) to becoming a man to whom the Lord Himself later gave the name "Israel" (which means "prince of God").

In order for the spiritual to connect with the natural there must be a point of entry. Getting something from heaven to the earth requires a gate, a place of transaction and transfer. The house of God is that gate and today's house of God is the Church. We are the gateway through which God's divine transfer of power can be released into our cities to bring about transformation. We must be careful, however, and not be asleep like Jacob was and miss seeing when God is moving.

In his dream Jacob saw a ladder with angels ascending and descending. The next time we see the phrase "angels ascending and descending" in the Bible, it occurs in reference to Jesus (John 1:51). Jesus Christ is the fulfillment of Jacob's ladder. He touches both heaven and earth. A ladder is something we use when we need something higher than we can reach. Jesus helps us reach something we couldn't reach before. He becomes the ladder that connects heaven and earth where angels ascend and descend. He becomes the point of transaction that establishes the gate of heaven so that the gates of hell cannot prevail against His Church. Our walls are salvation, our gates open up with praise and He establishes the Church as a place of divine transaction.

The Power of Truth

When the time is right and God releases a Word of truth (and *all* of God's Words are true), with that release comes the equalization of truth. This means that whoever works with that truth has the divine authority to transfer power. They have the capacity to make a power shift. We live in a day of shifting power. Why is power shifting all over the world? Because God has spoken. A divine transaction has taken place, yet much of the Church is asleep, not realizing that we are in a time of power shifting as never before in history.

Let me give you an example. The civil rights movement in America was a tremendous power shift because those who were thought to be powerless moved the mountains of law and social convention and changed the system. Our tendency is to think that power resides in majorities, position, and money. It doesn't. Most of the people involved in the civil rights movement possessed none of those things. What they did possess, however, was the *real* source of power—truth. By acting on the truth they possessed, a power transfer occurred and the lay of the social landscape in America was changed forever.

At the time, many who occupied the traditional seats of power in America opposed the civil rights movement. People with money, position, prestige, influence and well-organized political machines did everything they could to stop it. So did many unofficial "power" groups such as the KKK and other white supremacist organizations who fought the movement tooth and nail. Arrests, intimidation, terrorization and outright violence were used in an effort to contain it, but to no avail. The time was right. A Word of truth was released. Power shifted to the powerless and the heart of American society was transformed.

What made the difference? One side was working with truth and the other side was working with a lie. Ultimately, lies never outlast the truth. They may hold sway for a time while people are asleep to what God is doing or playing like children in the marketplace while power transactions are taking place above their heads. All it takes for change to occur is for someone who "has ears to hear" to pick up on the truth that has been released and act on it. Millions of ordinary "someones" heard that truth and said, along with Dr. Martin Luther King, Jr., "I have a dream…" They went forth in the power of that dream and the lies entrenched in American culture could not stand against them. That's the power of truth.

Mahatma Gandhi was in a similar situation. Although he was not a Christian, Gandhi was deeply impressed by the example of Jesus' holy life and by the moral force of His teachings. He was also a lawyer trained in the legal tradition of the British, who ruled his nation, India, and whose government and society were thoroughly socialized with Christian moral and social values. Gandhi heard the same truth that energized Martin Luther King a generation later and knew that with organized nonviolent civil disobedience, India could be freed from British rule and gain its independence. He was right because truth was on his side.

Evil will never overcome good. The gates of hell will never prevail over the gate of heaven. Truth can't be defeated by beating it down, blowing it up or locking it in jail. Truth cannot be killed. All truth is God's truth. His Word is truth and the Bible says that God's Word will not return to Him void but will accomplish all that He pleases and will prosper wherever He sends it (Isa. 55:11). When God says He is ready to shift a thing, all we have to do is hear it and get with it.

A Generational Shift

Power is moving all around us even if we can't see it. We can't hear it either, unless we tune in with spiritual ears: "He that hath an ear, let him hear what the Spirit saith unto the churches" (Rev. 2:7). It's time for Christians to stop acting like children, playing in the marketplace while transactions take place overhead. We've got to quit thinking like slaves in Egypt when we're living in a generation of transfer. When God says, "I'm getting ready to transfer cities, I'm getting ready to transfer wealth, I'm getting ready to transfer generations," we can't afford to be sitting around like children with no understanding of the time and season we're living in.

Why sit we here until we die? We must act while the anointing is on us. We need to shift while the shifting is happening. We have to get in the water while the water is yet troubled (John 5:1-4). Power is being transferred and we need to be part of it if we hope to transform our culture.

A generational shift is coming to the people of God. It has already happened in the secular marketplace and the Church needs to understand the time and season that we are in. In recent years the focus in secular American culture has shifted from idealism to realism.

Years ago, Americans watched TV for idealism. We wanted to see shows that portrayed life the way we *wanted* it to be: "The Brady Bunch," with nine people living harmoniously in one happy house; "The Partridge Family," happily traveling in that multi-colored bus and singing everywhere; "Father Knows Best" and "Leave It to Beaver," where the father was always wise (and always in a tie!) and the mother was always sensitive and compassionate; "Adam 12," with two nice, white, clean cut police officers doing a nice job for everybody. We wanted to see all of life's problems neatly resolved in a thirty-minute time segment.

A generational shift has occurred. Now our focus is on realism. Instead of "Fantasy Island" we have "Survivor"; instead of "Gilligan's Island" we have "Lost"; instead of "Ozzie and Harriet" we have "The Osbourne's"; instead of "American Bandstand" we have "American Idol"; instead of "Adam-12" we have "Cops." Car commercials used to focus on images of a shining vehicle that was showroom perfect. Then the car companies discovered that Americans aren't interested in what the vehicles look like on the showroom floor; we want to see what they're like on the road. Now the ads show cars, trucks and SUVs bouncing over dirt roads, driving through storms, and getting splattered with mud. Today we Americans demand nitty-gritty, down-and-dirty *realism*!

Who hasn't seen the memorable commercials of the Strong's padlock being shot through with a rifle bullet and still working? Or the Timex commercials where a Timex watch is plunged underwater or thrown out of an airplane to demonstrate that it "takes a lickin' and keeps on tickin'?" Or the Samsonite commercials where their suitcases are dropped from airplanes or stomped on and thrown about by gorillas to show how they keep their shape?

A generational shift has occurred. Life is not a showroom. Sometimes it gets dirty. Rarely can we solve our problems in a tidy thirty-minute time segment. Yet, in an age of realism, many churches still live, teach, and preach in a fantasy land of idealism with no knowledge or recognition that a shift has even taken place.

Once we in the Church truly understand the power of our product, we will stop trying to preach to the "Bradys" and the "Partridges" and the "Cleavers" and the "Nelsons" and start reaching the *real* people who live in *real* families with all their *real* problems and dysfunctions. Contrary to what many in our culture believe, we Christians have a four-wheel-driving, getting-through-the-mud, take-a-lickin'-and-keep-on-tickin'-kind of faith that will always get us through. We have a faith that can be stepped on but never stopped; a faith that can be slammed against the wall and will keep coming back. *And the folks in our secular culture need to know about it!*

Faith and Authority

One reason people in the secular culture are not attracted to the Church is because they perceive Christians as people of faith but who lack authority, and absence of authority makes the Church illegitimate (or at least irrelevant) in their eyes. Although erroneous, this is an honest perception considering that so many of the Christians they see or know *live* as though they have no authority.

The lifestyles of many Christians in America today are virtually no different from those of their non-Christian neighbors. Because of either ignorance of their faith due to biblical illiteracy or erroneous teaching in their churches, they live with little or no expectation of God ever doing anything significant in their lives. They anticipate future glory in heaven but look for none on earth. Powerless Christians constitute powerless churches and a powerless church impresses no one.

This is *not* the kind of faith Jesus taught and modeled. Authority permeated everything He said and did. No one in His day had ever seen the like and they noticed the difference: "And it came to pass, when Jesus had ended these sayings, the people were astonished at his doctrine. For he taught them as one having authority, and not as the scribes" (Matt. 7:28-29). When Jesus taught it was clear immediately that He spoke not from mere academic knowledge but as an authoritative source.

He imparted that same authority to the Church, implemented through the Holy Spirit. The problem is that so many Christians either don't know it or don't believe it.

A proper understanding of authority produces a faith that releases power. Consider the account in Matthew chapter 8 of Jesus and the centurion:

> *⁵And when Jesus was entered into Capernaum, there came unto him a centurion, beseeching him, ⁶And saying, Lord, my servant lieth at home sick of the palsy, grievously tormented. ⁷And Jesus saith unto him, I will come and heal him. ⁸The centurion answered and said, Lord, I am not worthy that thou shouldest come under my roof: but speak the word only, and my servant shall be healed. ⁹For I am a man under authority, having soldiers under me: and I say to this man, Go, and he goeth; and to another, Come, and he cometh; and to my servant, Do this, and he doeth it. ¹⁰When Jesus heard it, he marvelled, and said to them that followed, Verily I say unto you, I have not found so great faith, no, not in Israel. ¹³And Jesus said unto the centurion, Go thy way; and as thou hast believed, so be it done unto thee. And his servant was healed in the selfsame hour* (Matthew 8:5-10, 13).

If Jesus offered to come to your house would you decline? The centurion did. He felt unworthy to have someone as righteous and holy as Jesus enter his home. More importantly, the centurion did not need Jesus' physical presence because he understood authority. As a centurion he had soldiers under him and officers above him, so he knew authority from both ends. He obeyed the orders of his superiors without question and the soldiers under his authority obeyed his orders in the same way.

Because of this understanding, the centurion recognized the authority that resided in Jesus; an authority that extended even to the realm of physical disease. That is why he said to Jesus, "Speak the word only, and my servant shall be healed." His understanding of authority aroused in him a faith that confidently expected something to happen, and that faith released power. After marveling at the simplicity and depth of the centurion's faith Jesus said, "Go thy way; and as thou hast believed, so be it done unto thee." The centurion's servant was healed that very same hour.

The centurion understood the power of a word spoken from a place of authority; that you don't have to be present where the word was spoken in order to receive the effects of that word. The four leprous men outside the city of Samaria discovered the same truth. Faith informed by authority bridges the gap of distance and time between a divine Word spoken and our action. A word spoken from a place of authority shifts power even outside the realm of the ones who are present to hear it.

True power does not reside with those who hold high positions; neither is it found with people of wealth or political influence. True power lies with the people who dare to take a step in line with the Word they have heard from God and pull it into their region. That is a power transfer.

Prayer Releases Power

Power shifts also occur when the people of God pray. The twelfth chapter of Acts presents a dramatic example of the power that can be released through prayer.

¹Now about that time Herod the king stretched forth his hands to vex certain of the church. ²And he killed

James the brother of John with the sword. ³And because he saw it pleased the Jews, he proceeded further to take Peter also. (Then were the days of unleavened bread.) ⁴And when he had apprehended him, he put him in prison, and delivered him to four quaternions of soldiers to keep him; intending after Easter to bring him forth to the people.

⁵Peter therefore was kept in prison: but prayer was made without ceasing of the church unto God for him. ⁶And when Herod would have brought him forth, the same night Peter was sleeping between two soldiers, bound with two chains: and the keepers before the door kept the prison. ⁷And, behold, the angel of the Lord came upon him, and a light shined in the prison: and he smote Peter on the side, and raised him up, saying, Arise up quickly. And his chains fell off from his hands. ⁸And the angel said unto him, Gird thyself, and bind on thy sandals. And so he did. And he saith unto him, Cast thy garment about thee, and follow me. ⁹And he went out, and followed him; and wist not that it was true which was done by the angel; but thought he saw a vision. ¹⁰When they were past the first and the second ward, they came unto the iron gate that leadeth unto the city; which opened to them of his own accord: and they went out, and passed on through one street; and forthwith the angel departed from him. ¹¹And when Peter was come to himself, he said, Now I know of a surety, that the Lord hath sent his angel, and hath delivered me out of the hand of Herod, and from all the expectation of the people of the Jews. ¹²And when he had considered the thing, he came to the house of Mary the mother of John, whose surname was Mark; where many were gathered together praying. ¹³And as Peter knocked at the door of the gate, a damsel came to hear-ken, named Rhoda. [14]And when she knew Peter's voice, she opened not the gate for gladness, but ran in, and told how Peter stood before the gate. [15]And they said unto her, Thou art mad. But she constantly affirmed that it was even so. Then said they, It is his angel. [16]But Peter continued knocking: and when they had opened the door, and saw him, they were astonished. [17]But he, beckoning unto them with the hand to hold their peace, declared unto them how the Lord had brought him out of the prison. And he said, Go show these things unto James, and to the brethren. And he departed, and went into another place (Acts 12:1-17).

Peter was in jail…but the church was praying. James the brother of John had just been executed and it looked like Peter would be next…but the church was praying. By all appearances power lay in the hands of King Herod…but the church was praying. The Church is the gate of heaven, the place of transaction where power transfer occurs. The church was praying…and power shifted.

It was the middle of the night and Peter was asleep. Reminds you of Jacob, doesn't it? An angel appeared in Peter's cell, smacked him on the side and said, "Get up." Peter was in a place where power was shifting and he couldn't afford to sleep or he would miss it. The angel led Peter to the gate leading into the city, which opened by itself. Peter was so out of it that he thought all of this was a vision. Nevertheless, he was walking in line with a Word that he hadn't even heard spoken—the Word released from heaven because the church was praying. The word for Peter's deliverance was spoken and the gate to the city opened of its own accord…because it was *time* for it to open. The church was praying…and power shifted.

Peter made his way to the house where the church was gathered in prayer. They were "astonished" to see him, which suggests that even though they had prayed for Peter's deliverance, they did not expect it so soon or in the manner in which it occurred. After explaining what happened, Peter departed and went into hiding for a time.

Herod had the power…or did he? Not long after Peter's miraculous deliverance, Herod delivered a speech to the people of Tyre and Sidon. His eloquence so impressed them that they heaped praises on the king:

> [22]*And the people gave a shout, saying, It is the voice of a god, and not of a man.* [23]*And immediately the angel of the Lord smote him, because he gave not God the glory: and he was eaten of worms, and gave up the ghost.* [24]*But the word of God grew and multiplied* (Acts 12:22-24).

King Herod, the man who thought he had the power, died at the hand of the Lord's angel but the Word of God (and the church that proclaimed it) continued to grow and multiply. The church prayed…and power shifted.

Like Peter, we can be asleep when God is moving or we can be awakened to what He is doing. When we begin to walk and to work in line with what God is doing, he will open the gates of our cities, a power transfer will be made, and the Church will be empowered to engage and transform the secular culture with the power of the gospel of Jesus Christ. Once the power shifts, the gates of hell will not be able to stand and those held in bondage by the powers of darkness will be led into the light of life and freedom.

SECTION FOUR

Preparing for a New Apostolic Generation

While others play games in the
marketplace of ideas and philosophies
these have come to transact
serious business.

Chapter Eight

The Emerging Apostolic Generation

We are living today in perhaps the most exciting and most significant time in history since the first century. Many modern-day theologians who study current affairs and compare them with New Testament times are saying that what they see shaping up in our own day is a movement of Christ through His Church that will be larger and greater than what happened in the Book of Acts. There is growing evidence that we are entering a new apostolic age where the ministry gifts of God are going to function in greater power and authority than at any time in the past 2000 years. New areas are going to break open where the gospel of Jesus Christ has never penetrated before. Areas that have been cold and resistant to the move of God for decades—perhaps centuries in some cases—are going to break wide open through the power of the Holy Spirit. This is already starting to happen in some places.

With God beginning to move so mightily in the earth to bring about His plan of the ages, it is vitally important that we become informed as believers about what God is doing and prepare ourselves and our churches to coordinate with Him so that we can be available as vessels and instruments for His use. Nothing would be more tragic than for a church to miss its moment—its destiny—due to ignorance of God's activities and subsequent lack of preparedness.

In this emerging apostolic generation we can expect to see a significant increase of signs, wonders, and miracles accompanying the proclamation of the gospel and the ministry of the Church. Many new and strong churches will be established. The arising of this new apostolic age will usher in a great world wide revival unlike anything that has occurred before. Some signs of this have appeared already.

Another sign that God is at work doing a new thing is the increase of activity by the powers of darkness. Whenever the light increases, the darkness increases also in an effort to blot it out. This is one reason why we are witnessing today an unprecedented attack on traditional biblical and moral values. The traditional family is under assault as never before with legalized abortion killing millions of unborn babies in the womb every year and with radical activists attempting to redefine marriage to include same-sex couples. Never before in the history of mankind has any society defined or recognized marriage as anything other than the union of one man with one woman. Religious freedom is being undermined everywhere, even in America and particularly with regard to Christians. In general, persecution of Christians worldwide is on the rise, particularly in Muslim countries.

It would be easy to look at such trends and become fearful or discouraged. We must remember that this increase in satanic activity is in response to the increase of God's activity in the world. As God enables and empowers His people in new and fresh ways and as Christ mobilizes His Church to go on the offensive in a new apostolic age, the forces of the enemy are going to fight back ferociously. In the end they will lose because, as we saw in the last chapter, "greater is he that is in [us] than he that is in the world" (1 John 4:4). In Christ we are "more than conquerors" (Rom. 8:37) and He promised long ago that the gates of hell would not prevail against His Church (Matt. 16:18).

With this new apostolic generation we are going to see history repeated but in greater form. What the Lord did before He is getting ready to do again, only this time it will not be with only twelve people but with *thousands*. The apostles are coming and their arrival will herald a new day when a freshly empowered Church will move forth in new confidence and authority to tear down strongholds, change climates and images, and shift power on an unprecedented scale.

If we are to prepare ourselves and our churches for the arrival of this new apostolic generation, we need to know what to look for. How will we recognize the apostolic anointing when we see it? What evidence will reveal that apostolic work is underway? Answering these questions is important if we want to coordinate and flow with what God is doing in this day and in this hour. Our ability to identify genuine apostolic ministry is also important because it will help us recognize *false* apostles when they appear—and they will.

Genuine apostles will bring a "finishing anointing" to the Church; an anointing to complete what the Church began 2000 years ago; namely, proclaiming the gospel of Christ to all the world. This "great commission," Jesus promised, will be accomplished before the end comes. Before Christ returns, every nation and every people group on earth will hear the gospel. Ours may very well be the generation that witnesses the completion of that task.

The office of apostle is the first listed office of the five-fold ministry that Christ gave to the Church to build it to fullness and maturity. All five offices—apostle, prophet, evangelist, pastor and teacher—are necessary for the full functioning of the Church. Under the apostolic anointing, the Church will move out to reap a harvest not of 30-fold or 60-fold, but of 100-fold (Mark 4:3).

With this in mind, let's examine the characteristics and evidence of the apostolic anointing so we can recognize it in our midst.

Tangible Results

One defining characteristic of the apostolic ministry is the supernatural ability to see *tangible results*. In other words, apostles do not deal just in concept but also have a supernatural anointing to be able to identify something as being the result of apostolic ministry. As Paul wrote to the Corinthian Christians, "Am I not an apostle? am I not free? have I not seen Jesus Christ our Lord? *are not ye my work in the Lord?* If I be not an apostle unto others, yet doubtless I am to you: for *the seal of mine apostleship are ye in the Lord* (1 Cor. 9:1-2 emphasis added).

Paul could point to the Corinthians as the sign and the seal of his apostleship. The presence and continuing growth of the church in Corinth were tangible results of Paul's apostolic ministry. If anyone questioned Paul's apostolic credentials or anointing (and some people did), all he had to do was point to the Corinthian church and say, "There's your evidence."

Apostles have a special anointing from the Holy Spirit not just to teach principles but to build something up from nothing by faith and by the virtue of God. Thus was Paul able to go into areas where the gospel had never been preached, winning thousands of Gentiles to Christ from paganism, planting church after church and training and appointing elders and overseers. Paul, like the other apostles, had a supernatural grace to see tangible results.

This is not to say that Christians who do not have the apostolic anointing should not expect results from their ministry. Every Christian has the Spirit of God residing within and therefore possesses the capacity to do the "greater works" that Jesus talked about in John 14:12. Jesus said that we would do greater works than He because He was returning to His Father and would send the Holy Spirit to dwell in us forever. It is by the anointing and power of the indwelling Spirit that we would do these "greater works."

All Christians, therefore, operate in the Spirit of God, but those anointed for the offices of the five-fold ministry have a particular measure of grace above and beyond the norm to equip them for the particular offices they fill. God always equips us adequately for the assignments He gives us. We all have a measure of anointing, a measure of authority, and a measure of grace that we stand in. Apostles and others in the five-fold ministry have a different measure than the rest because they have a governing capacity over the house of God.

Apostles are specially gifted to see tangible results. One of the reasons that God is releasing them into the earth today is because He's getting ready to bring us into the 100-fold increase.

Witness to the Resurrection of Christ

The apostolic ministry in the first century church gave witness to the resurrection of Christ with great power: "And with great power gave the apostles witness of the resurrection of the Lord Jesus: and great grace was upon them all" (Acts

4:33). One of the things that needs to be restored to the Church today is the ministry gift that gives witness to the resurrection of Christ not only in word but also in *power*. Don't get me wrong; there is incredible power in the Word of God because it is the Word of the living God and "is quick, and powerful, and sharper than any twoedged sword, piercing even to the dividing asunder of soul and spirit, and of the joints and marrow, and is a discerner of the thoughts and intents of the heart" (Heb. 4:12). In the early church, however, a clear sign of apostolic ministry was when great power for signs, wonders, and miracles accompanied the preaching of the gospel as conformation of the truth of the words spoken. Such too will be the hallmark of the emerging apostolic generation. These new apostolic people and churches will attest to the resurrection of Christ in both word and power.

Supernatural Anointing for Breakthrough

Apostles also have a supernatural anointing for *breakthrough*. They possess a particular measure of spiritual authority that empowers them to achieve spiritual breakthrough in places or situations that have proven impervious to others. Modern day apostles can, like Paul, go into areas where the gospel is either unknown or strongly resisted and bring breakthrough in that place in a way nobody else can. They can go into an environment hostile to Christianity, a place with a powerful and pervasive negative spiritual climate and change that climate by the power of their anointing.

Under this same anointing, apostles can also bring breakthrough to God's people. In certain areas where, because of the negative environment, even Christians may be bound up by tradition or religion or unclean spirits and unable to walk fully in the freedom of God, apostles can go in and preach and blast away in the spirit until breakthrough comes. One of the reasons the apostolic ministry is such a blessing to the people of God is that it keeps blasting in the spirit until it creates an open heaven which produces an atmosphere of blessings.

Apostolic ministry helps bring freedom. The nature of the breakthrough anointing is such that an apostle can go into an area and without any prior knowledge discern what strongholds are present that are binding and enslaving the people. Then, like a laser zeroing in on a target, they zero in on those strongholds and preach and blast away until those obstacles fall and people are set free. Even in areas where other five-fold offices may receive a cool reception, apostles can go in and pull down strongholds, dispute with the people about their mindset, aggravate their traditions, challenge them to another way of life and establish the Kingdom of God in those places—all because of the breakthrough anointing.

Supernatural Ability to Gather Large Armies

Another characteristic of apostolic ministry is its supernatural ability to gather large armies together. Acts 2:41 says that on the day of Pentecost after the outpouring of the Holy Spirit and after Peter's inspired preaching that 3000 people were saved. When Paul and Barnabas preached in Antioch of Pisidia, almost the entire city came out to hear them (Acts 13:44). More than two dozen times in the Book of Acts the term "multitude" is used in connection with apostolic ministry. When apostles show up and preach, it causes such a shaking in the spirit until multitudes gather to hear the Word.

Some ministries in the Church are "hidden" ministries in the sense that they generally operate behind the scenes and away from public view. The ministry of intercessory prayer is a good example. Apostolic ministry, however, is by nature out front and public. Because of the high visibility of apostolic people, God gives them a special grace to withstand pressure, criticism and even persecution without knuckling under. Paul described this special grace perfectly when he wrote:

> *⁸We are troubled on every side, yet not distressed; we are perplexed, but not in despair; ⁹Persecuted, but not forsaken; cast down, but not destroyed; ¹⁰Always bearing about in the body the dying of the Lord Jesus, that the life also of Jesus might be made manifest in our body. ¹¹For we which live are alway delivered unto death for Jesus' sake, that the life also of Jesus might be made manifest in our mortal flesh. ¹²So then death worketh in us, but life in you* (2 Corinthians 4:8-12).

Paul and the other apostles knew a special grace that enabled them to stand and endure far beyond their own human capacity. Whether it is functioning to readjust people's thinking, to bring order, to instill doctrine or to bring corrections in the body of Christ, the upfront nature of apostolic ministry requires the special ability to stand firm without wavering.

Apostolic ministry is characterized also by the strength of its voice, not so much in physical delivery necessarily as in the supernatural authority behind it. Paul himself acknowledged to the Corinthians his own "weakness...fear, and...much trembling" and that his speech and preaching did not come "with enticing words of man's wisdom, but in demonstration of the Spirit and of power" (1 Corinthians 2:3-4). It is this authoritative strength of voice that enables an apostle not only to preach and achieve breakthrough but also to draw multitudes of people together, substantial new armies of warriors and servants of the Lord.

Supernaturally Impart and Activate Spiritual Gifts

Part of the authority apostles possess is the authority supernaturally to impart and activate spiritual gifts within the hearts of people as well as to train those who function in those gifts. Paul wrote to the Christians in Rome, "For I long to see you, that I may impart unto you some spiritual gift, to the end ye may be established" (Rom. 1:11).

As with all of the five-fold ministry offices, apostolic ministry is an edifying ministry whose purpose is to establish, strengthen, and build up the church into maturity in Christ. Impartation and activation of spiritual gifts are part of this edifying process. New Testament apostles gathered believers together, taught them doctrine, brought breakthrough and imparted spiritual gifts, often by the laying on of hands, as Paul mentions in Second Timothy 1:6: "Wherefore I put thee in remembrance that thou stir up the gift of God, which is in thee by the putting on of my hands." Acts 8:5-17 tells of Phillip's preaching and producing converts in Samaria, after which Peter and John came in an apostolic role and laid hands on the new converts so they could receive the Holy Spirit. In Acts 19:1-7, Paul laid his hands on twelve new believers, upon whom the Holy Spirit came and who "spake with tongues and prophesied."

It was common in the New Testament church that whenever somebody had a mission to fulfill or was entering into a new ministry that apostles would lay hands on the individual and impart and activate spiritual gifts and abilities that were not present in that individual before. This impartation would empower that person to fulfill the mission or calling that he or she had received from the Lord. The apostles, who were responsible for the establishment and welfare of the churches, did not simply appoint an elder or overseer over a congregation and say, "Okay, you figure it out." Instead, they would lay hands on that overseer and impart to him the spiritual gifts that he would need for the pastoral work which he was now undertaking.

In addition to imparting spiritual gifts, apostles have the gifting and authority to train those under them in the use of the gifts they have received by apostolic impartation. Because the apostolic gift is an ordering gift, apostles have the ability to discern dormant gifts, callings and destinies in the lives of people. One thing that happens under an apostolic covering is the proper alignment, realignment and placement of spiritual gifts in the body of Christ. Apostles have a divine grace from God to see naturally where people belong in the functioning of the local faith community.

Many churches are out of order because some people are "higher" in authority and function than they should be while others are lower than they should be and their gifts are underutilized. Under an apostolic ministry, the proper order is restored. Those who are too high for their gifting or in the wrong place are repositioned and those who should be higher are pulled to a higher level. This is not a matter of anybody being better than anybody else. It is simply a matter of placing people where they have been gifted to serve so that everyone can reach his or her fullest potential and so the entire body of Christ can operate at greater effectiveness. All of this is by the sovereign choice of the Holy Spirit as administered through the apostolic ministry.

There are many highly gifted yet underutilized people in the Church today whom God wants to release in a more perfect measure so that they don't function just in a gift but in an impartation and a flow of the Spirit so that they can become fully effective with the gifts God has given them. In our own day God is releasing an apostolic ministry because He has a whole army of people that He wants to fill up, fire up, and power up in the Holy Spirit. This is one reason why so often we see many gifted people around apostolic ministry. Apostles attract gifted people because they have the ability to train those people and to bring them into their fullness and their measure in the work of God's Kingdom.

A Special Measure of Revelation

A sixth characteristic quality of apostolic ministry is that it has a special measure of revelation. Apostles often receive by revelation things that cannot be fully derived through study. While this is true to a certain extent for any believer studying the Bible under the illumination of the Holy Spirit, divine revelation is present to a more pronounced degree with apostolic people. Even when study is involved, they receive more insight through the Spirit than they could get by using a concordance or other study aids along with their Bible.

Once again, Paul provides a good biblical example:

> *²If ye have heard of the dispensation of the grace of God which is given me to you-ward: ³How that by revelation he made known unto me the mystery; (as I wrote afore in few words, ⁴Whereby, when ye read, ye may understand my knowledge in the mystery of Christ) ⁵Which in other ages was not made known unto the sons of men, as it is now revealed unto his holy apostles and prophets by the Spirit; ⁶That the Gentiles should be fellowheirs, and of the same body, and partakers of his promise in Christ by the gospel⁷Whereof I was made a minister, according to the gift of the grace of God given unto me by the effectual working of his power* (Ephesians 3:2-7).

Paul states plainly in verse 5 that apostles and prophets receive by the Spirit of God revelation into the "mystery of

Christ" that was not revealed to people of earlier ages or, by implication, to people in the present age who do not carry the apostolic anointing.

Although the Old Testament was written primarily by people in the prophetic ministry, the New Testament was composed mainly by apostles or by someone very close to them and under the direct influence of their teaching. Part of the reason for this is because apostolic ministry has the grace not only to receive revelation but also to interpret Old Testament Scripture in the light of contemporary events. The relevance of this for today is that the emerging apostolic ministry has the ability to receive revelation from God and in the light of that revelation speak the purposes and will of God into modern society.

A Supernatural Flow of Miracles

Apostolic ministry is characterized also by the supernatural flow of miracles that surrounds it. Acts chapter three tells how a man lame from birth was healed by the apostles Peter and John. Speaking from his apostolic authority, Peter said, "Silver and gold have I none; but such as I have give I thee: In the name of Jesus Christ of Nazareth rise up and walk" (Acts 3:6). In Acts 9:33-34 Peter heals a man named Aeneas who has been bedridden for eight years, saying to him, "Jesus Christ maketh thee whole: arise, and make thy bed." They understood that they had a measure of authority. The Book of Acts also tells how sick people would line the side of the road where Peter was passing so that when his shadow fell on them, they were healed (Acts 5:15).

Similar miracles occurred in the presence of Paul: "And God wrought special miracles by the hands of Paul: So that from his body were brought unto the sick handkerchiefs or aprons, and the diseases departed from them, and the evil spirits went out of them" (Acts 19:11-12).

Miracles always surround apostolic ministry. It was that way with the New Testament apostles and it is that way with today's emerging apostolic generation. We need apostolic ministry to rise up in the earth today and prove God's Word through signs and wonders following. God wants to have apostolic churches where even if the pastor can't lay hands on people, the altar workers or other members can bless people and believe God with them on their jobs, or pray with them in the hospital or in the neighborhood and see miracles come about. True apostolic ministry is always surrounded by miracles.

Supernatural Authority Over Demonic Influences

Closely related to the supernatural flow of miracles is the apostolic ministry's supernatural authority over demonic influences. Acts 5:16 says in relation to the ministry of the apostles in Jerusalem, "There came also a multitude out of the cities round about unto Jerusalem, bringing sick folks, and them which were vexed with unclean spirits: and they were healed every one." In Philippi Paul cast a "spirit of divination" out of a slave girl, destroying the livelihood of her masters who made money from her "ability." This incident precipitated Paul's arrest, along with Silas, and they ended up in jail where an earthquake set them free and led to the conversion of the Philippian jailer and his family (Acts 16:16-34). Philip's preaching ministry in Samaria resulted in many people who were possessed by unclean spirits being delivered by the apostle (Acts 8:5-8).

Apostolic ministry also engages in warfare against territorial spirits that hold sway over different cities and regions. In First Corinthians 15:32 Paul speaks of having "fought with beasts at Ephesus," a probable reference to ruling spirits over that great city. Apostles have a special grace and anointing to confront and displace territorial spirits.

Release of Supernatural Judgment Against Wickedness

Apostolic ministry also has the authority to release supernatural judgment against wickedness. Part of this anointing is the ability to judge ministries: to discern the truth and whether or not someone is functioning under an anointing from God. Not everyone who claims to be called by God is called by God and not every ministry that carries the name "Christian" is Christian. Apostles have a unique capability to discern the difference.

Apostles also often can discern deception. When Ananias and Sapphira sold some land, kept some of the money for themselves and brought the rest as an offering, claiming it was the full amount, Peter discerned through supernatural insight that they were lying. Peter pronounced judgment on them for lying to the Holy Spirit and Ananias and Sapphira both dropped dead (Acts 5:1-11). In his apostolic authority Peter released judgment on wickedness.

Acts 13:6-12 tells of Paul's encounter with Elymas, a Jewish sorcerer and false prophet. Paul and his companion Barnabas were sharing the gospel with a local governor named Sergius Paulus, who was sincerely interested in hearing the Word of God. Elymas opposed their message at every turn and tried to sway the governor away from the faith, bringing down on his head a divine judgment through the lips of Paul: "O full of all subtlety and all mischief, thou child of the devil, thou enemy of all righteousness, wilt thou not cease to pervert the right ways of the Lord? And now, behold, the hand of the Lord is upon thee, and thou shalt be blind, not seeing the sun for a season. And immediately there fell on him a mist and a darkness; and he went about seeking some to lead him by the hand" (Acts 13:10-11). Sergius Paulus was so astounded by this blatant display of divine power that he became a believer immediately.

Apostles may also release judgment against someone when the safety of God's people is at stake. In First Corinthians 5:1-5 Paul pronounces judgment on a man in the Corinthian congregation who was living in sexual sin with his father's wife: "For I verily, as absent in body, but present in spirit, have judged already, as though I were present, concerning him that hath so done this deed, In the name of our Lord Jesus Christ, when ye are gathered together, and my spirit, with the power of our Lord Jesus Christ, To deliver such an one unto Satan for the destruction of the flesh, that the spirit may be saved in the day of the Lord Jesus" (1 Cor. 5:3-5).

The New Testament church understood better than we do what it meant for someone to be "delivered unto Satan." Essentially, it means he was put out of the church. To be part of the church was to be under an apostolic covering and thus protected from satanic attack. Someone who was put out of the church was also removed from under the apostolic covering and so became vulnerable to the enemy. Paul didn't perform some big ritual of judgment and condemnation; he simply said to the offending man, in effect, "You're outta here."

The purpose of this action was not only to protect the integrity of the church and the other believers but also to bring the offender to his senses and to repentance and restoration. In that sense, then, being delivered over to Satan was an act of mercy and love aimed at effecting redemption for the sinner.

Apostolic judgment will also be a part of this emerging generation because all over the world today are forces and enemies that oppose the gospel and those who proclaim it. In many places there are voodoo spirits or Islamic spirits or Hindu spirits or Buddhist spirits that come out in Christian meetings and evangelistic campaigns and try to curse the ministers and scare the people away and do all sorts of other ungodly and unclean things. The day is coming when apostolic people will go into such places and in the authority of their anointing release judgment against those who oppose the Word so that the gospel can proceed unhindered to reach into the hearts of those who need to hear it.

Supernaturally Strengthen and Oversee Ministries

One of the most significant and important functions of apostles is to supernaturally strengthen and oversee ministries. Whenever genuine apostolic ministry comes to a church, that church is strengthened. Prophetic ministry may say to a church, "This is where you will build"; apostolic ministry comes in and starts laying bricks. When you're around apostolic ministry you can't help but get built up; that's part of its function. Paul said, "According to the grace of God which is given unto me, as a wise masterbuilder, I have laid the foundation, and another buildeth thereon. But let every man take heed how he buildeth thereupon" (1 Cor. 3:10).

Paul did not build on someone else's work but laid his apostolic foundation in the lives of people. By laying a good and solid foundation, he set the stage for others to come and finish the good work by building up the church. This does not mean that Paul left the churches he founded to their own devices. He would plant a church, train up and appoint leaders, lay hands on them and impart and activate spiritual gifts. Throughout his ministry he continued to strengthen them and give oversight through prayers, letters and, when possible, personal visits.

Apostolic ministry strengthens and oversees the churches so the people of God don't get tired and weary and beaten up and worn out, and helps them stay on the straight path theologically and doctrinally so they don't slip into error and false teaching.

A Supernatural Supply

Finally, apostolic ministry is characterized by a supernatural supply. Of course, every believer has access to the supernatural supply of God, but this is even more so with the apostolic ministry because of the resources it requires to accomplish God's purposes. Whenever God calls apostles to a place to push for breakthrough, He will supply them with everything they need to do the job. Apostles need a great supply because they are called to do things beyond what others in the Church do. Just as gifted people are attracted to and fathered by apostolic ministry, so God attracts different people of different means and resources to sow into apostolic ministry because they sense a call into something larger than what they have been living for.

Acts 16:14-15 tells of Paul planting the first church in Europe in the city of Philippi. His first convert in that city was a prosperous woman named Lydia, who was a seller and dealer in purple fabric, a very expensive commodity. After her conversion and that of her family, she felt led of God to open her home as a meeting place for the new church and her personal resources in its support. God put it in Lydia's heart to bless Paul's apostolic ministry so they could get a church started. Lydia was a woman of means with enough wealth, connections, and ability to help get the new Philippian church off the ground.

When apostolic ministry comes, God begins to bless people in a greater measure so that they can be a blessing into that apostolic ministry. People who get connected with it have a different measure of blessing that can come into their own lives. God then begins to bring people together and cause what they give to multiply. He begins to convert people of wealth who have been putting their resources toward the wrong things or people who have used their positions for wrong things or people who have used their talent for wrong things.

One of the things I believe we will see in this emerging apostolic generation is people in the sports world, the music world, the movie industry, and the business world who have reached the top of their professions only to discover that they are unhappy and unfulfilled, who will then begin to come into contact with apostolic ministry. As a result, their lives will be transformed by the power of the gospel. They will give their lives to Christ, and their resources, connections, finances, notoriety, and influence will shift from the world to the Church. Since all resources ultimately belong to God, He knows how to turn them to whatever purposes He desires.

***

A great power shift is coming and I believe we will see it in our own day. Strongholds are going to fall, climates are going to be altered, and images are going to be changed as the people of God own the truth that we have received from the Lord and lay claim to our rightful place as possessors of the land in His name. In the power of the new apostolic anointing we will confront our culture and see it transformed as a great worldwide revival sweeps from nation to nation and people to people.

Because God has called this present generation to so much, and because the vision is so large, and because the enemy is fighting so hard, God is going to reach right into the place where the devil thought he had built up a secure kingdom and upend it. People whom the devil has used to pervert, deceive, and mislead a generation will be claimed by the new apostolic ministry, which will grab them and shake them and bring them into the Kingdom of God. We are seeing the emerging of a new apostolic people—a people who are saying to God, "Do what You want to do, anyway You want to do it, and use us in Your plan to reach and transform our culture."

Power is shifting. God is releasing a new generation of apostolic people and churches; *power shifters* who will advance in His name and in His anointing to shake not only modern culture and its institutions, but the very foundations of hell itself. Apostolic leaders are reshaping the spiritual landscape even now. Mysteries are being revealed, boundaries are being broken, walls are tumbling, and the limitations are being removed. As a result of their spiritual architecture strong houses are being raised up filled with a company of people who, empowered and activated by apostolic fathers, are shifting the power.

You and I will live to see nations that have been closed to the gospel open up and break forth into amazing revival. People groups all over the world who have been held under poverty, oppression, and bondage will experience new found freedom and deliverance. God's people will rise to be the head (decision makers) and not the tail.

As God opens ancient doors to revelation and keys of access are granted we will move in a dimension that is beyond human ability and find a flow of the Spirit that causes unlikely places to be sought out for its spiritual value.

There is a shift taking place can you feel it? Power is being transferred do you know it? It is happening all around you do you desire it? You have the power to shift your world will you do it?

**"Arise, shine; for thy light is come,
and the glory of the Lord is risen upon thee."**
Isaiah 60:1

Books by Michael Pitts

Living On the Edge

Making the Holy Spirit Your Partner

Breaking the Assignment of Spiritual Assassins

Breaking Ungodly Soul Ties

A Dictionary of Contemporary Christian Words & Concepts

Help! I Think God is Trying to Kill Me

Don't Curse Your Crisis